The Little Book of Oil Painting SECRETS

The Little Book of Oil Painting SECRETS

A World of Practical Art in Your Pocket

Scott Maier

DAVID & CHARLES
— PUBLISHING —

www.davidandcharles.com

Contents

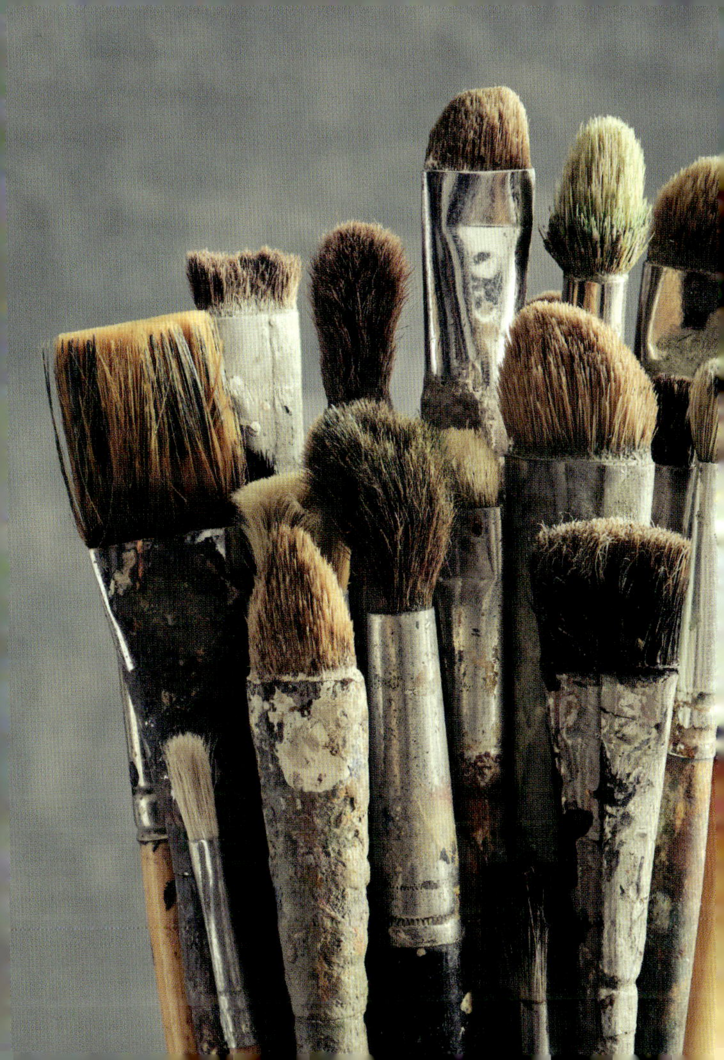

Introduction

For a long time, there have been lots of assumptions about painting in oils: that you have to work for years, mastering other mediums before graduating to the chosen paint of the masters. It's something to aspire to—it's messy, expensive, and demands a level of skill that seems impossibly distant. But what if that's all wrong? What if the very things that make oil painting seem so "difficult" are precisely what makes it perfect for beginners?

"Sunrise over Horsetooth" 2022, oil on panel.

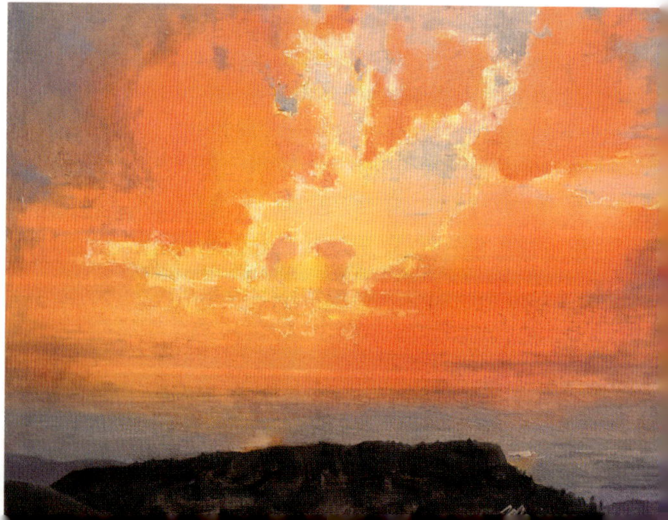

Qualities identified as barriers aren't obstacles. They are advantages. The slow drying time isn't an inconvenience, it's a gift. It gives a beginner time to think, reflect, react, and see what's happening on the canvas without the pressure of a ticking clock.

And the ability to scrape away paint and start over? That's not a sign of failure, it's an extraordinary safety net. It dramatically lowers the stakes of making a mark and creates an environment where experimentation isn't just possible, it's the most valuable tool for your growth as an artist.

This book is built around that philosophy of discovery. Having painted with oils for more than 30 years, I've learned from countless "failed" paintings that the medium isn't about perfection, it's about possibility. Through trial and error, I've come to realize that while there is no single "correct" way to paint, there are fundamental characteristics of oil paint that are empowering when understood.

In this book, we will explore these fundamentals—how to mix color, layer paint, and work with a brush—as a foundation for your own artistic goals. As you become more comfortable with the mechanics, you will discover your unique way of working, whether that's a more refined and controlled approach or a loose, exploratory one.

My goal is to lay the groundwork for that journey. I'm offering guidance from the perspective of someone who has made a career's worth of mistakes! You'll still experiment and make a mess, of course, but in the process, you'll gain confidence and clarity. It's an exciting journey, and it starts now.

CHAPTER 1

Essential Materials

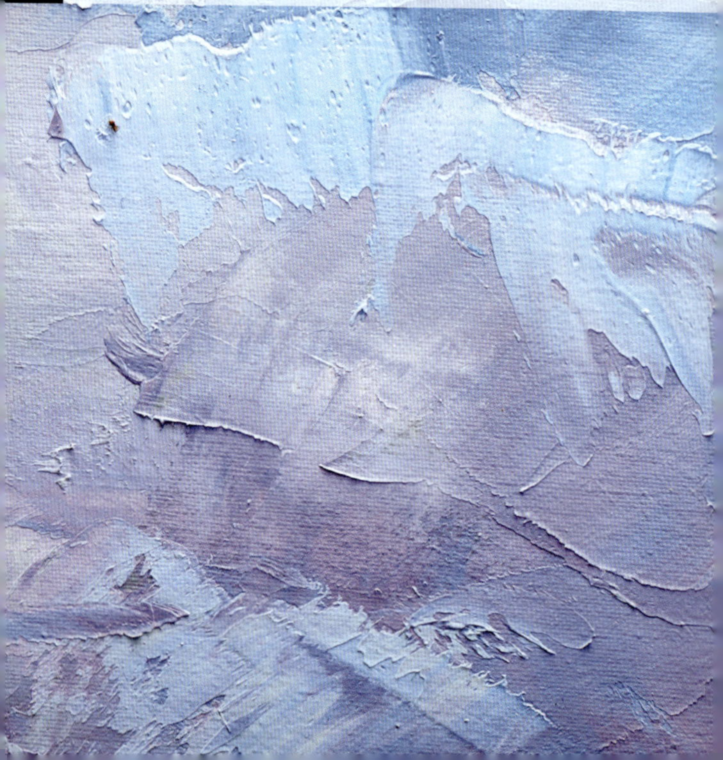

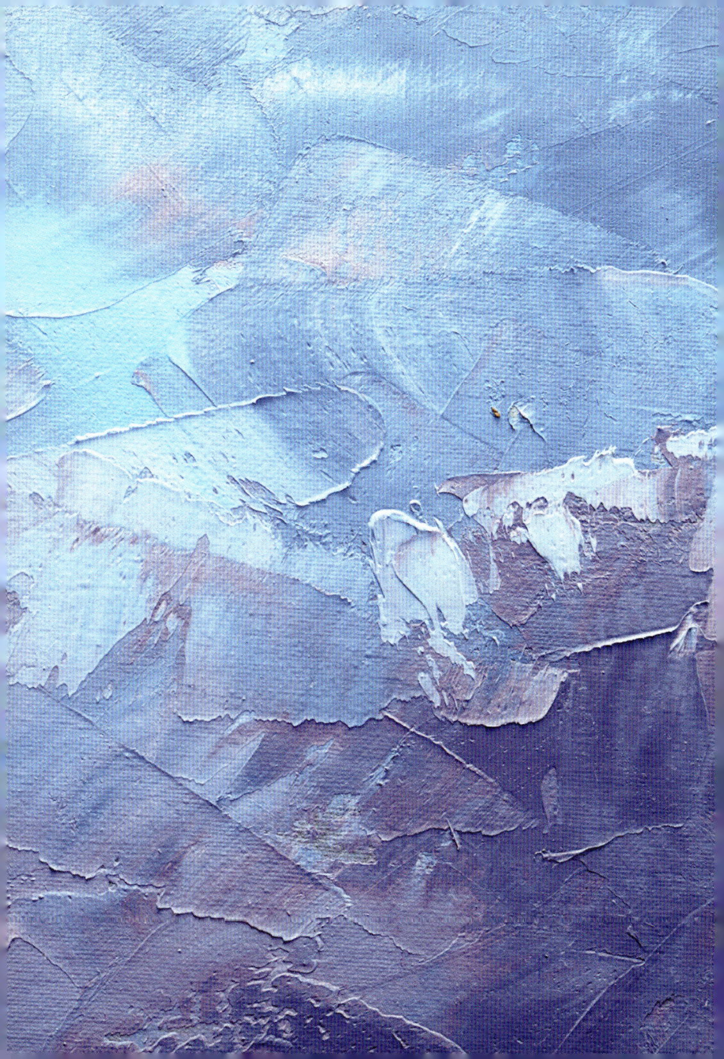

An Artist's Toolkit

Taking the first creative step means assembling your tools. While the world of art materials can seem complex, the truth is that a powerful painting practice is built on simple, well-chosen basics. This isn't about acquiring everything, it's about understanding what truly matters.

This chapter will help demystify the process. We will walk through the tools and materials—the specific paints, brushes, surfaces, and mediums—that form the core of a functional and flexible studio. Think of this as your comprehensive guide to building a toolkit that empowers you to get straight to the most important work: painting.

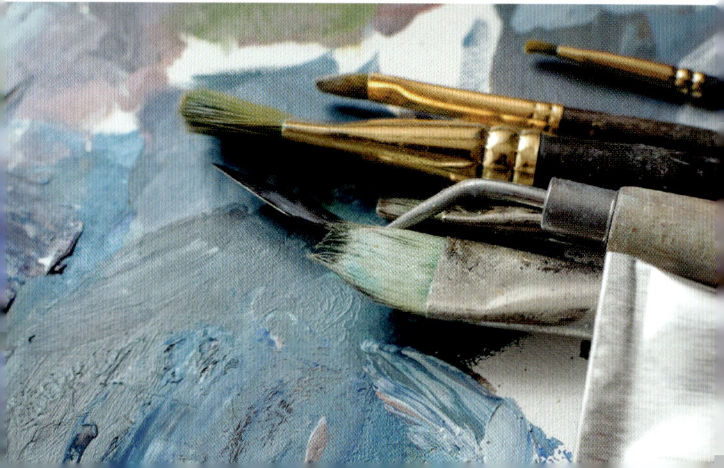

Oil Paints

Oil paints are pigments mixed with an oil (usually linseed oil). They are known for their rich colors, ability to blend smoothly, and longer drying time, which gives you lots of flexibility. Oil paints are available as "Student Grade" and "Artist Grade." Student-grade paints are more affordable, and while they might have a bit less pigment than artist-grade paints, they are perfectly good for learning and practicing.

You don't need a massive set of paints. A limited palette of essential colors will serve you well when starting out because it promotes the learning of basic color mixing. Try to get a warm and cool version of the three primary colors (red, yellow, and blue) plus white.

My recommendations are: Cadmium Red Light (warm red), Quinacridone Magenta (cool red), Cadmium Yellow Deep (warm yellow), Cadmium Yellow Light (cool yellow), Ultramarine Blue (warm blue), Phthalo Blue (cool blue), and a good-sized tube of Titanium White.

Artist-grade oil paints offer a high pigment load and a smooth consistency. As you gain experience, consider switching to artist-grade paints for more precision with color and brushwork.

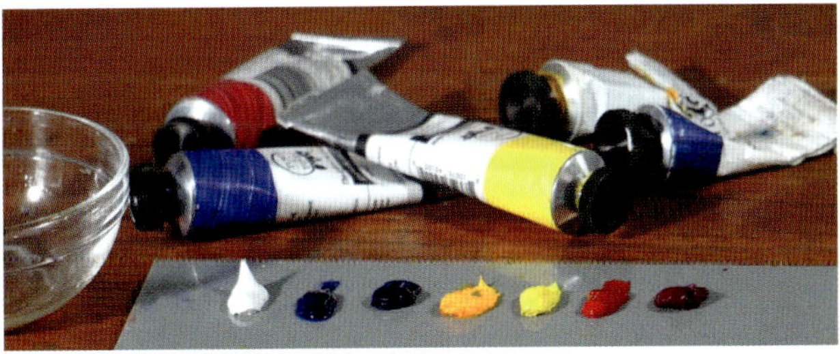

Brushes

For oil painting, brushes usually have longer handles and come with different types of bristles. You'll mostly see natural hair (often hog bristle) and synthetic brushes. Hog bristle brushes are stiff and great for holding thicker paint and creating texture, while synthetic brushes are often softer and work well for smoother application and blending. It's best to start with a few basic shapes and sizes to see what you respond to. A couple of round brushes (good for lines and details), a couple of flat brushes (great for blocking in larger areas and creating straight edges), and maybe a filbert or two (a flat brush with a rounded end, good for blending and softer edges) in a few different sizes (a small, medium, and large) will give you a great range to work with.

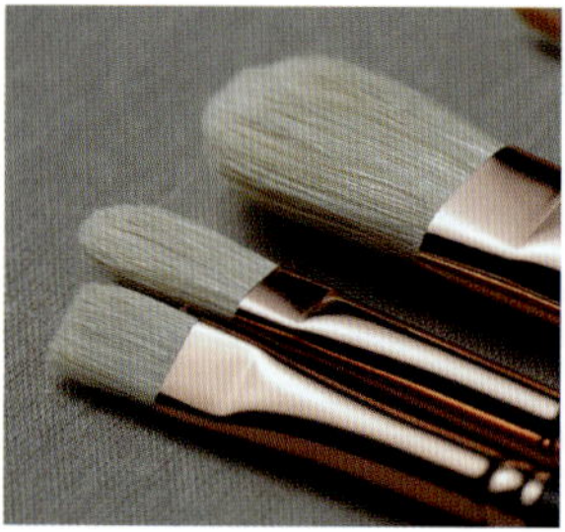

Natural bristle brushes are stiffer and great for texture. Consider starting with a larger filbert (right) and flat (left) brush in your initial set.

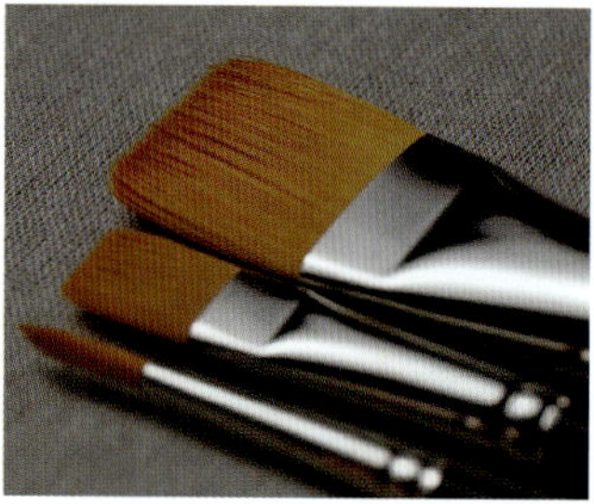

Synthetic brushes are softer and work well for blending and smooth brushwork. Consider starting with a variety of flats (right) and round (left) brushes in your initial set.

Surfaces

The most common surface for oil painting is canvas. You'll find canvas already stretched over wooden frames (stretched canvas) or glued onto rigid board (panels). Canvas panels are generally more affordable and easier to store, making them great for practice and studies. You can also paint on specially prepared paper for oils, which is also very convenient for studies. Oil paint needs a prepared surface, (also called a ground), because the oil in the paint can eventually degrade the paper. This preparation is called gesso (pronounced "jess-oh"), a primer that seals the surface and gives the paint something to stick to. Luckily, most stretched canvases and panels are already gessoed and ready to go—look for labels that say "primed" or "acid-free."

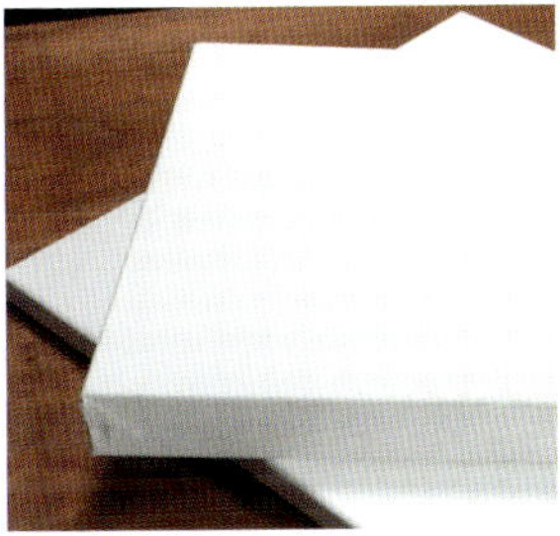

Stretched canvases are available in a variety of sizes and thicknesses, primed and ready to paint.

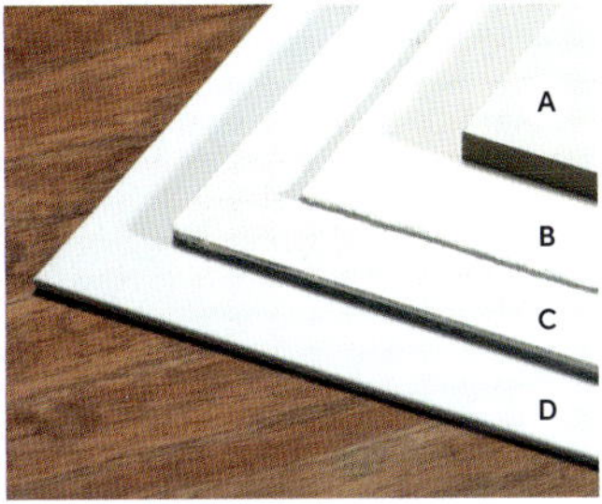

There are many alternative surfaces that are widely available, including hardboard (A), paper (B), canvas (C), and linen (D).

Mediums and Solvents

Sometimes you want to change the consistency of your paint, make it flow more easily, or control how fast it dries. That's where mediums (types of oil) and solvents come in. A simple rule for oil painting is using more oil thickens your paint, and using less oil or adding solvent will thin your paint. We'll explore this more in Chapter 4.

As a beginner, you don't need a wide variety of mediums. A basic drying medium can help speed up drying time if you're impatient, and often just using a little solvent is enough to thin your paint for initial layers. Solvents (like odorless mineral spirits or turpentine) are primarily used to thin paint and to clean your brushes. Odorless mineral spirits are a less toxic and less smelly option than traditional turpentine. The following is a quick guide to mediums to help you make the right choice for your work.

Among the most commonly used oil mediums are linseed oil, walnut oil, stand oil, and safflower oil. Each has their own viscosity, texture, and drying time.

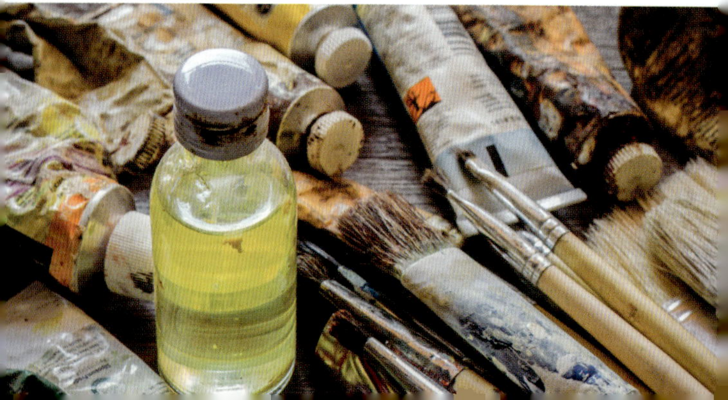

LINSEED OIL

The most common, relatively fast-drying oil derived from flaxseeds, versatile for various techniques but can yellow if overused.

STAND OIL

A thick, syrupy version of linseed oil that dries slowly, ideal for glossy finishes and glazes, but may need thinning.

WALNUT OIL

A lighter-colored oil that dries slower than linseed oil, excellent for blending and extended wet-in-wet work.

SAFFLOWER OIL

A pale, light-bodied oil with a slow drying time, good for wet-in-wet techniques and light colors, known for being less prone to yellowing.

POPPY OIL

A thin, slow-drying oil with transparent qualities, often used for whites and light colors, but could become brittle and crack over time.

A NOTE ON CONTAINERS

When pouring out your solvents and mediums, always reach for glass or metal containers rather than plastic or paper cups. Solvents are powerful enough to eat through many plastics and will soak right through paper, leading to spills and potential hazards. A glass jar is the safest option or even a metal brush washer with a tight-fitting lid. This not only keeps your workspace clean but also prevents evaporation, allowing you to reuse your solvent for future sessions.

Palettes

Your palette is simply the surface where you put your paints and mix your colors. Palettes come in different materials. Wooden palettes are traditional but need to be seasoned with a few coats of oil prior to painting. Glass palettes are easy to clean but can be fragile and heavy. Many beginners find disposable paper palette pads convenient—you just tear off the top sheet and throw it away when you're done! Choose a palette that gives you plenty of space to squeeze out your colors and, importantly, lots of room in the middle to mix paint.

Palette Knives

A palette knife is an essential tool for mixing colors on your palette. Its flexibility allows you to thoroughly blend your paints without muddying them. A basic diamond-shaped or teardrop-shaped palette knife with a little flex is perfect for getting started. It's also useful for creating texture effects, scraping, and building thick layers of paint (impasto).

Easels

While you can certainly paint with your canvas flat on a table, an easel holds your painting upright, allowing you to face your canvas directly and limit distortions while working. Painting vertically can also help prevent dust from settling on your wet paint and encourages you to step back and look at your painting from a distance as you work. You don't need a fancy studio easel to start. A simple tabletop easel or a lightweight tripod easel is perfectly fine for holding your canvas while you paint.

Palettes come in a whole host of shapes, sizes, and materials, including paper (bottom), wood (middle), and plastic (top).

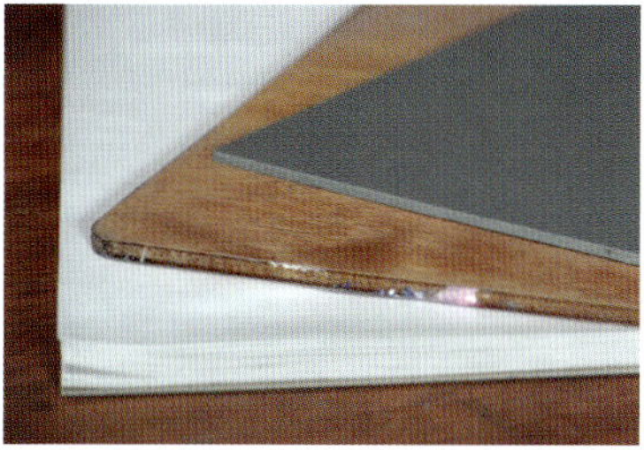

Palette knives are essential tools for the studio. Metal knives (left) are more sharp, stiff, and robust than plastic knives (right), but are also more expensive. Consider starting with a plastic knife and switching to metal as you gain confidence.

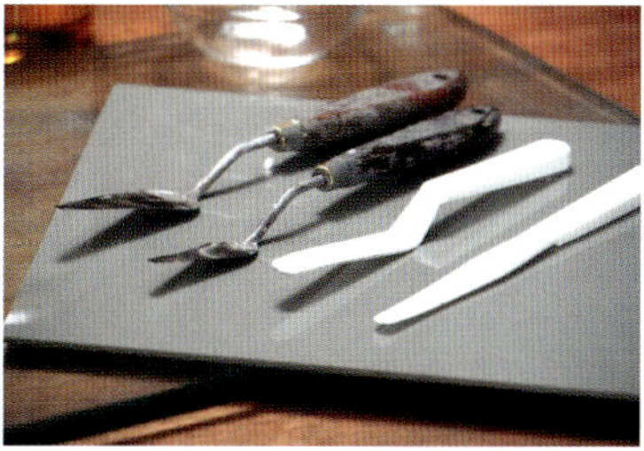

Easels come in a variety of shapes and sizes. A floor-standing "H Frame" easel like this one is a standard option for studio painting.

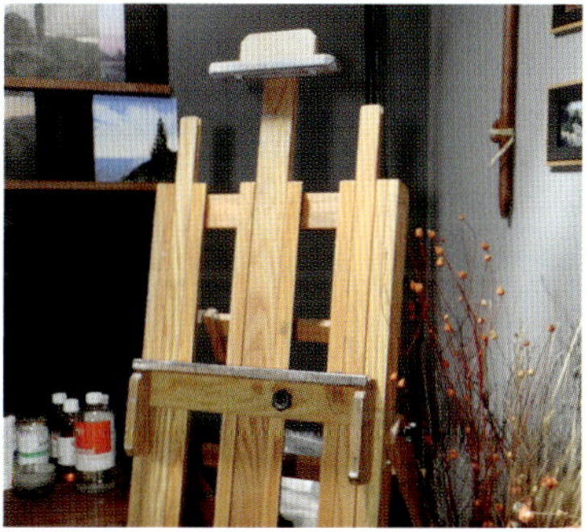

Establish a Clean-up Routine

After each painting session, take the time to thoroughly clean your brushes and wipe down the mixing area of your palette. To clean your brushes:

1. Rinse: rinse the brushes in your solvent to remove the bulk of the wet paint, then wipe them clean with a rag.

2. Wash: give the brushes a deeper cleaning at a sink using a dedicated brush cleaner or gentle soap and water. Work the soap into the bristles until the lather runs completely clear of any pigment.

3. Dry: the way you dry your brushes is critical for their longevity. To prevent damage, either hang them with the bristles pointing down or lay them flat. This simple step ensures that water and any remaining residue won't seep down into the ferrule (the metal band), where moisture can rot the wooden handle and dissolve the glue that holds the bristles, causing them to splay and shed.

A Note on Safety

Painting in oils is generally safe, but there are a couple of things to be aware of. First, when using solvents, it's important to have proper ventilation. Opening windows and using an oscillating fan to generate airflow can often be sufficient. Rags soaked in oil mediums, particularly linseed oil, can pose a very real fire hazard, as they generate heat as the oil dries. Putting them in the regular trash can cause the temperature to build to a point where the rags ignite. It's best to discard used oil rags in a metal, fireproof container and check the rules on safely discarding waste in your local area.

Let's Paint!

You've got your paint, your brushes, a surface to paint on, a place to mix, something to thin paint and clean brushes, and a tool for mixing. That's really all you need to get started. Don't feel pressured to buy everything at once or get the most expensive versions. A basic, carefully chosen set of materials is all you need to begin your exciting journey into oil painting. Gather your supplies, set up your space, and get ready to experience the magic of putting paint on canvas!

"Hay Bales" 2023, oil on panel.

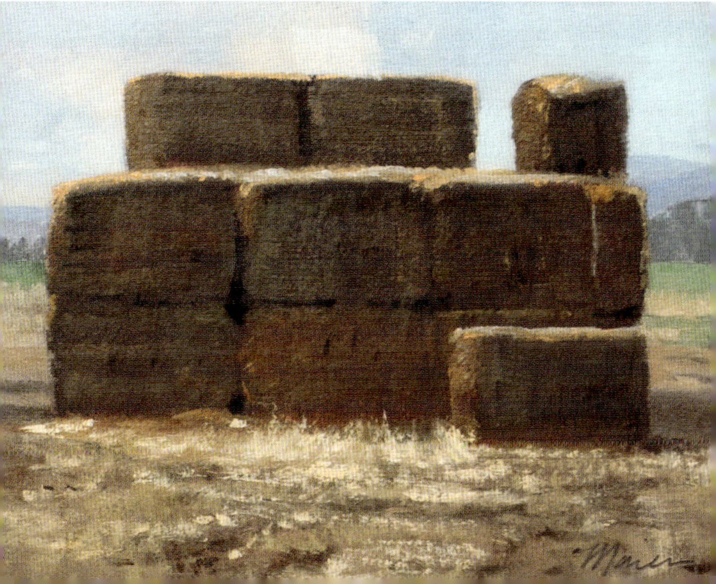

CHAPTER 2

Find Your Subject

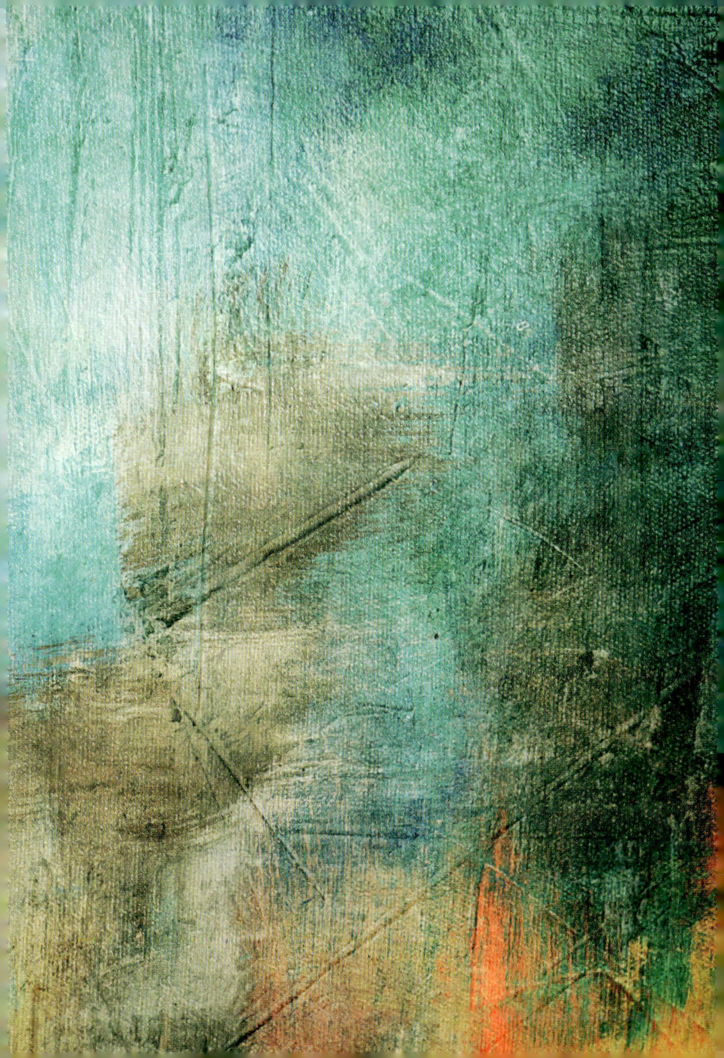

Choosing What To Paint

An important question every painter asks is, "What should I paint?". Let's be clear: there are no rules. A landscape can be a tranquil, realistic scene or an explosion of abstract emotion. A portrait can be a study in precise detail or a few bold, expressive strokes. Any subject can be approached in any style.

However, here is a powerful idea to consider as you begin: the subjects we choose are not passive. They have an active influence on our creative process. The subject itself challenges us to solve certain problems, to think in particular ways, and to use our materials in a manner that can shape our painting experience.

This changes the central question. It's no longer just "What do I like to look at?", but rather, "What kind of experience do I want to have at the easel? What kinds of problems do I want to solve?". Do you want the quiet, meditative experience of total control over light and composition? Do you crave the challenge of capturing a fleeting moment of light across a vast space? Are you driven by an intense curiosity about human emotion and character?

Here, we explore a selection of common genres that could align closely with your natural inclinations. By understanding what each path inspires, you can better choose the journey that will be most satisfying for you.

Landscape

Landscape painting is the art of commanding space—of capturing the power, light, and atmosphere of the world around you. Here, we learn the magic of perspective not as a rule, but as the tool to create light, atmosphere, and depth on a flat canvas. Faced with the complexity of nature, we also confront the skill of simplification: editing the chaos to compose a powerful, personal statement. This is a path for the artist with a deep connection to the outdoors, one fascinated by changing light and space.

"Landscape at Arleux-du-Nord," Jean-Baptiste-Camille Corot, 1871–74, oil on canvas, collection of The National Gallery of Art, London, bequeathed by Helena and Kenneth Levy, 1990.

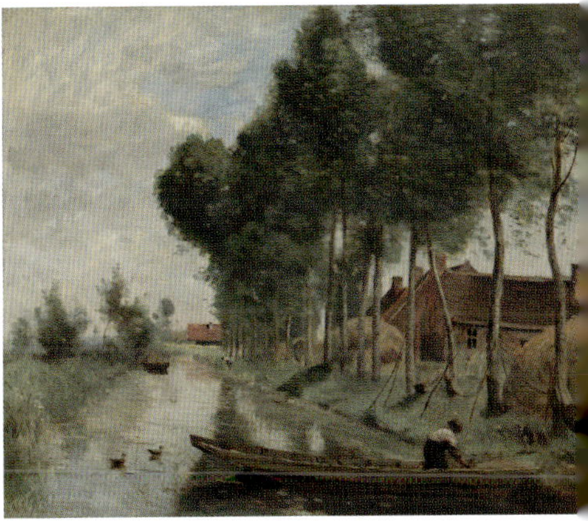

Still Life

Still life offers an opportunity for control. It is a private laboratory for becoming the sole director of light, form, and story. As we arrange objects, we focus on composition and the language of relationships. With full control over lighting, we learn precisely how light carves out form and dictates mood, translating the physical world—the rough skin of an orange, the flow of fabric—into the language of paint. This is a discipline for the patient observer exploring the relationship we create with objects.

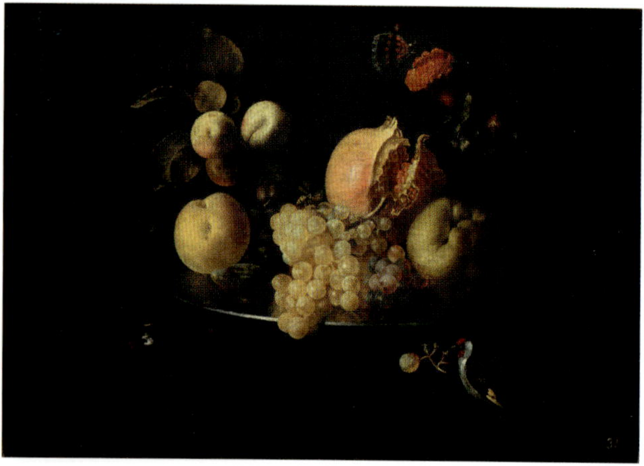

"Still Life with Fruit and Goldfinch," Juan de Zurbarán, 1639–40, oil on canvas, Museu Nacional d'Art de Catalunya, Barcelona.

Floral

Floral painting is the art of capturing fleeting beauty, inspiring intimacy and urgency. This subject is an opportunity to explore nuance and delicacy, forcing us to see and mix the hundreds of subtle color shifts within a single petal. It's an opportunity to practice a dynamic range of brushwork, from bold strokes to delicate marks, all in an effort to observe transient moments. This subject is for the artist captivated by intricate details, color, and texture.

"Sunflowers," Vincent van Gogh, 1889, oil on canvas, Van Gogh Museum, Amsterdam.

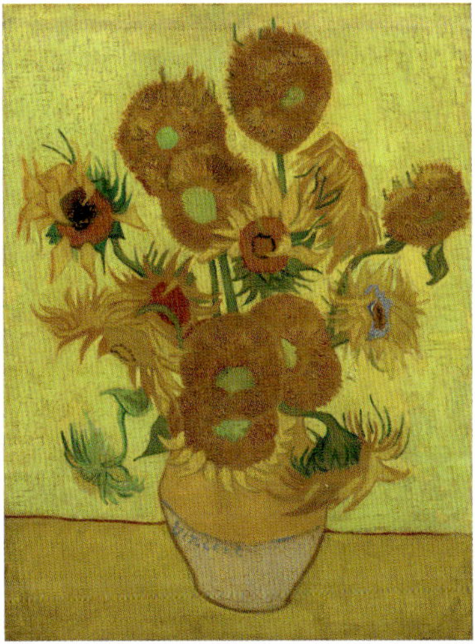

Portrait

Portraiture is a profound challenge: challenging the technical skills involved with capturing a likeness, as well as an understanding of abstract qualities that can express mood and emotion. While technical skill in anatomy is the entry point, the true work is becoming an empathetic observer. We learn to read the subtle language of a facial expression and mix the complex colors of skin to suggest a living presence. A great portrait is a dialogue that reveals something true about both artist and subject. This is a discipline for artists fascinated by people, relationships, and what it means to capture a likeness.

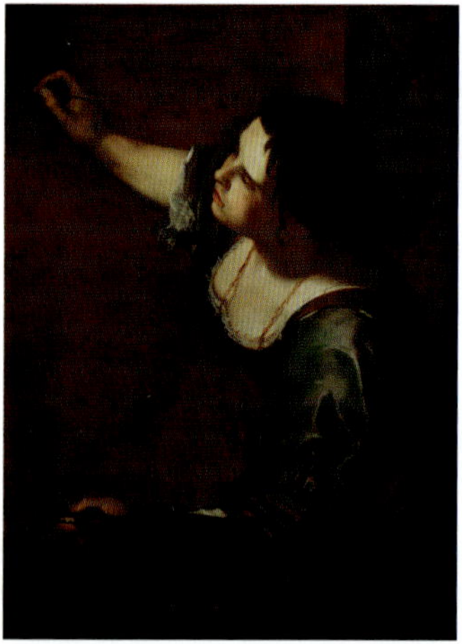

"Self-portrait as the Allegory of a Painting," Artemisia Gentileschi, c.1638-9, oil on canvas, Royal Collection Trust.

Architecture

Architectural painting is the art of exploring the structures we build and the spaces we inhabit. Here, we master the powerful logic of perspective to render buildings with a convincing sense of solidity. We become students of light as it carves across façades and casts sharp, graphic shadows that define form. This path appeals to the artist fascinated by design and order, who sees beauty in the interplay between structure and the natural light that envelops it.

"View of a Street," Mikkel Mandt, 1845, oil on canvas, National Museum of Art, Architecture and Design, Oslo.

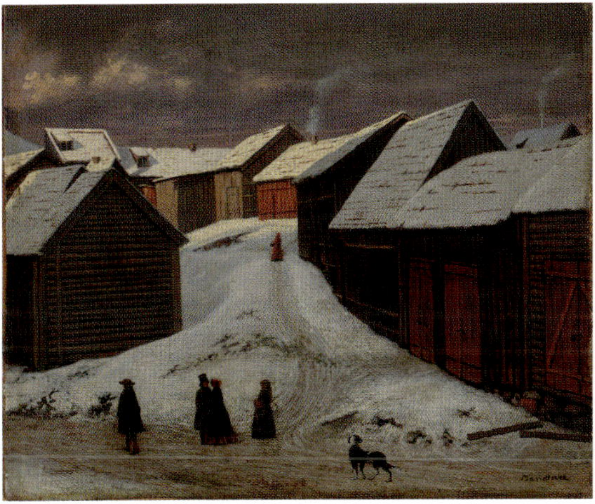

Animals and Wildlife

Wildlife painting shares qualities inherent in both portraiture and landscape painting. It encourages us to become a student of life, learning anatomy as well as environment. It challenges our skills with brushwork, process, and rendering texture—from soft fur to rough scales—to convey a living presence in its natural habitat. This is a path for artists with a profound connection to, and curiosity of, the animal kingdom. One who enjoys expressive, detailed work and careful study.

"Study of a Bighorn Ram," Albert Bierstadt, unknown date, oil on canvas, private collection.

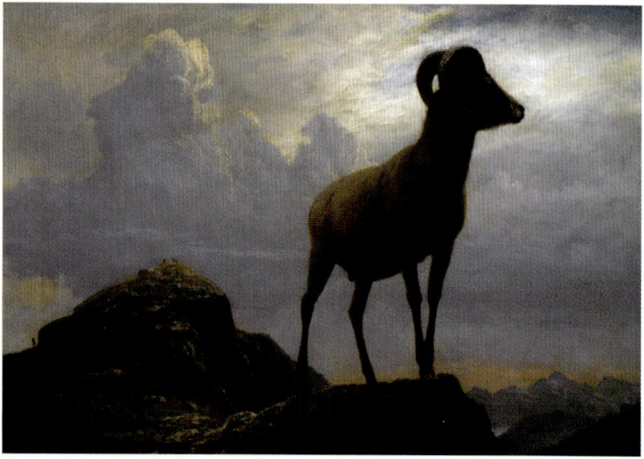

Abstraction

Abstraction offers the ultimate freedom: liberation from the literal world to use the pure language of color, shape, and texture as our subject. Without a recognizable subject, we rely entirely on composition and color to create emotional impact. Color becomes our vocabulary; texture becomes our voice. Abstract art is a deep dive into the nature of our materials and a direct, personal dialogue with the viewer. Abstraction is for the innovator who wants to convey an internal state rather than an external reality.

"Composition VIII," Wassily Kandinsky, 1923, oil on canvas, Guggenheim Museum, New York City.

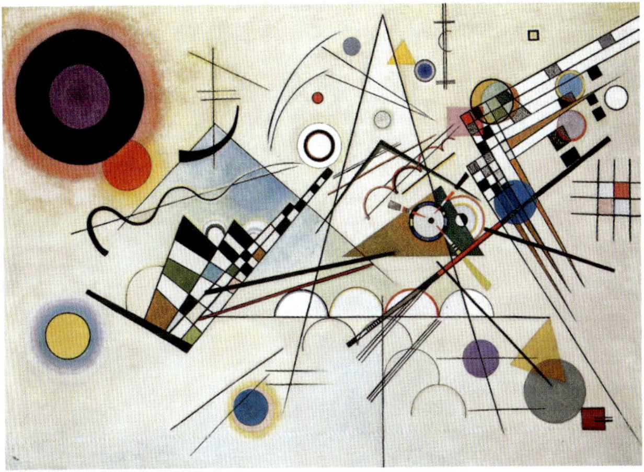

Artist Insight

Rosa Bonheur's artistic success challenged the limitations society placed on 19th-century women. To capture life-like animal anatomy on her large canvases, she obtained a special government decree to wear men's attire and granting her entry to male-only venues, like butcher shops and cattle markets. At home, she maintained a private zoo of creatures, including big cats, providing a steady supply of live models for her detailed studies.

"Wild Cat," Rosa Bonheur, 1850, oil on canvas, Nationalmuseum, Stockholm.

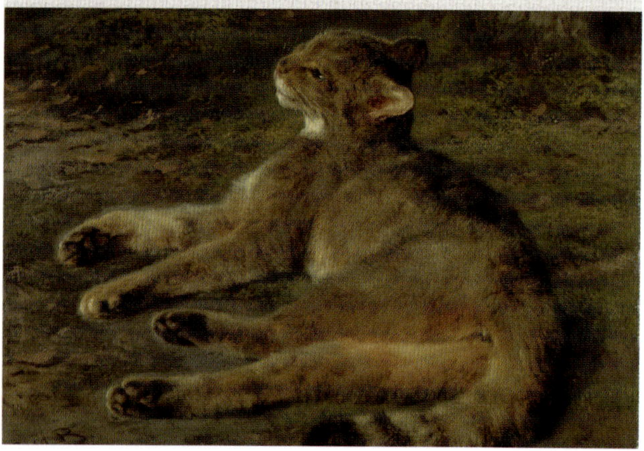

Paint What Pleases You

As you consider these genres, don't just ask what you want to paint. Ask what you want to discover. Which challenges excite you? Which way of seeing resonates with your spirit? Your subject isn't just a thing to render, it's the catalyst for the kind of artist you will become.

"Vermont" 2021, oil on panel.

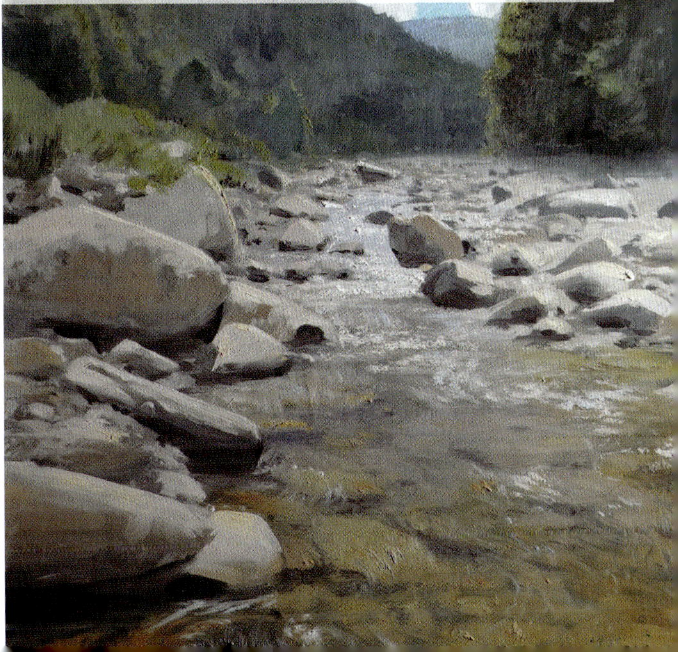

CHAPTER 3

Find Your Voice

Discovering Your Style

One of the biggest sources of anxiety for a new artist is the pressure to have a "style." Let's set that concern aside right now. Your unique artistic style is something that will emerge naturally, an authentic signature that will develop the more time you spend painting. You don't need to find a style—your style will find you.

So, why look at these common genres at all? We are using our familiarity with these basic approaches not as boxes to fit into, but as tools to help us discover our own connection to the painting process. Each approach—be it Realism, Impressionism, or Abstraction—promotes a mindset, a set of decisions, and the use of techniques that influence our overall painting experience.

As you've read in the previous chapter, you need to shift your thinking. The question is not, "Which style should I use?" but rather, "What kind of experience do I want to have at the easel?". Are you drawn to the experience of meticulous focus? The thrill of spontaneous expression? The intellectual challenge of communicating an idea? By understanding what each approach inspires and what it offers in return, you'll better understand your personal connection with the painting process.

Realism

Realism aims to make paintings look as close to real life as possible through accuracy and refinement. This involves closely observing the subject to capture every detail, focusing on correct lights and shadows to show form, managing sharp and soft edges, and mixing colors precisely. An extreme version, trompe l'oeil, attempts to fool the viewer's eye completely. This style sharpens observation skills, improves drawing accuracy, and refines your control over color mixing and smooth paint transitions. Realism is a good fit for artists with a sharp eye for precision who enjoy the challenge of controlling the medium and the sense of accomplishment in achieving accuracy.

"Trompe-l'oeil au portrait du chirurgien Le Cat," Gaspard Gresly, 1752, oil on canvas, private collection.

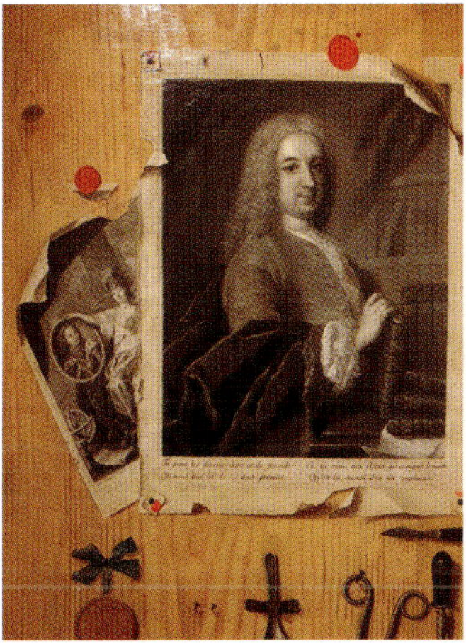

Impressionism

Impressionism captures the feeling of a moment, focusing on the effects of light and atmosphere rather than perfect detail. Often painting outdoors ("en plein air"), artists use direct, visible brushstrokes and place dabs of pure color side-by-side, letting the viewer's eye blend them. This approach inspires the simplification of subjects and a search for efficient brushwork, placing the right color, shape, and mark on the canvas to create the impression of the subject, rather than using strict, refined detail. Exploring this style develops a better eye for how light affects color, improves the ability to simplify a scene, and builds confidence with looser, more expressive brushwork. It appeals to artists inspired by natural light, who enjoy capturing quick moments and the energy of visible brushwork.

"Impression, Sunrise," Claude Monet, 1872, oil on canvas, Musée Marmottan Monet, Paris.

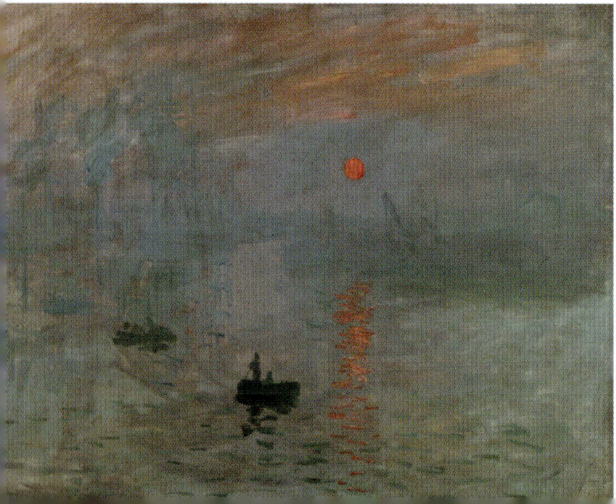

Symbolism and Expressionism

These styles prioritize expressing emotions and ideas over literal representation. Artists use objects as symbols and exaggerate shapes and colors to increase the emotional impact, focusing on inner feelings. The artist's personal vision is most important, and colors are chosen for their expressive power. Working in these styles inspires us to use color, line, and shape to deliberately communicate feelings and concepts. It also strengthens our ability to create compositions with emotional weight. This approach resonates with artists who are driven by emotion and storytelling, and are less concerned with the precision of realism.

"Anxiety," Edvard Munch, 1894, oil on canvas, Munch Museum, Oslo.

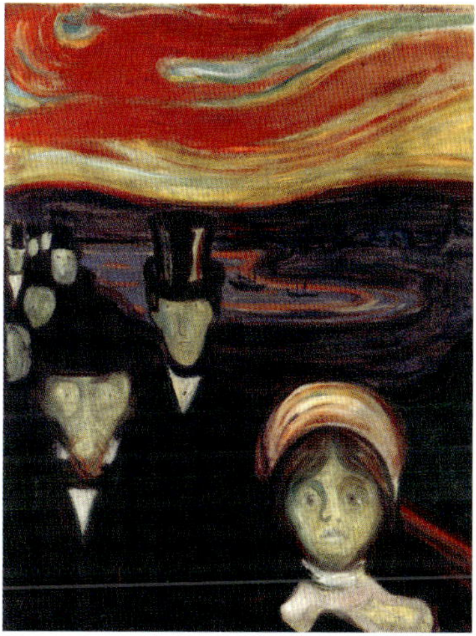

Surrealism

Surrealism dives into the world of dreams and the unconscious, creating illogical and bizarre scenes. Drawing inspiration from fantasies, artists create surprise by putting unrelated things together in unexpected ways. To tap into the subconscious, some use techniques like "automatism" (letting the hand move freely). Experimenting with Surrealism pushes us to think creatively and boosts our imagination, challenging us to find visual ways to represent unusual ideas. This approach attracts artists with strong imaginations who are fascinated by psychology and dreams, and enjoy blending observed and imagined realities.

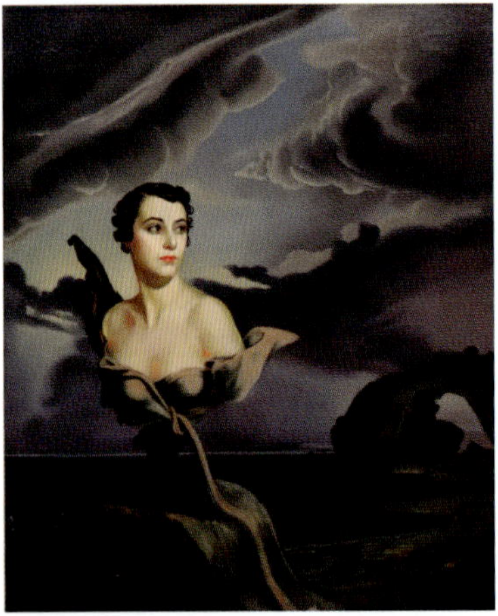

"Portrait of Loelia, Duchess of Westminster," William Acton, 1937, oil on canvas, private collection.

Abstraction

Painting abstractly is a move away from recognizable objects towards a focus on pure elements like color, shape, line, and texture. Artists use these elements expressively to create a direct emotional feeling or explore concepts like balance and energy. It offers complete creative freedom to invent, bend, and hijack the "rules" of painting. Working with abstraction encourages bold experimentation with paint application and the trusting of intuition. This style appeals to artists driven by pure visual expression, who enjoy exploring concepts and engaging the viewer in an open-ended conversation.

"Paysage aux toits Rouges," Chaïm Soutine, 1919, oil on canvas, private collection.

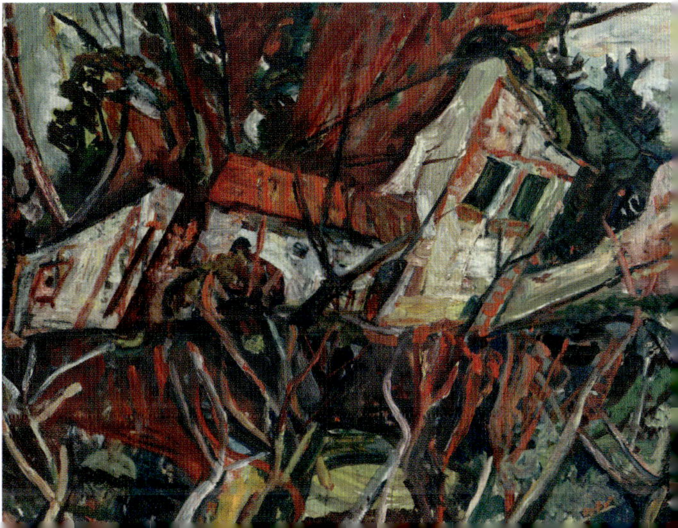

Artist Insight

Surrealist artist Max Ernst invented innovative techniques like "frottage" (rubbing) and "grattage" (scraping) to introduce elements of chance and unexpected textures into his artworks, stimulating his creative process. Ernst described discovering frottage in 1925 when observing the patterns of a worn wooden floor; he placed paper over it and rubbed it with a pencil, transferring the texture. He then applied this technique to various other materials like leaves, string, and seashells.

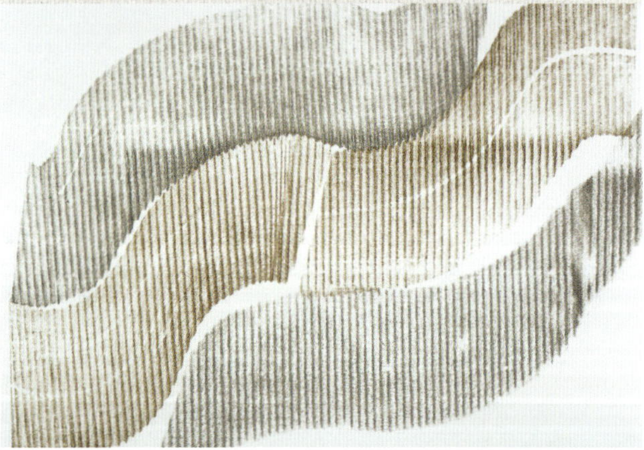

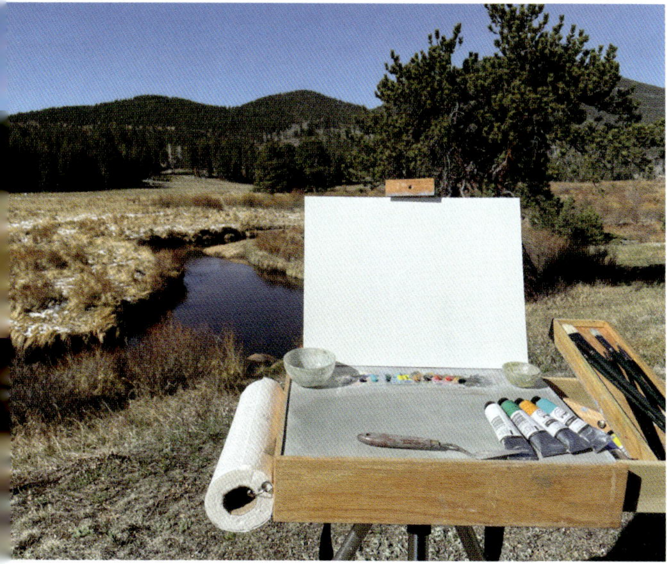

Finding Your Artistic Path

This has been a quick tour of painting styles. As you paint, notice what you enjoy most—capturing details, playing with color, or expressing feelings. Don't worry about choosing and committing to a style. Focus on the experience you want at the easel. The best way to find what fits is to experiment, observe your instincts, and practice. Your unique way of painting will emerge the more you work.

CHAPTER 4

Practical Techniques

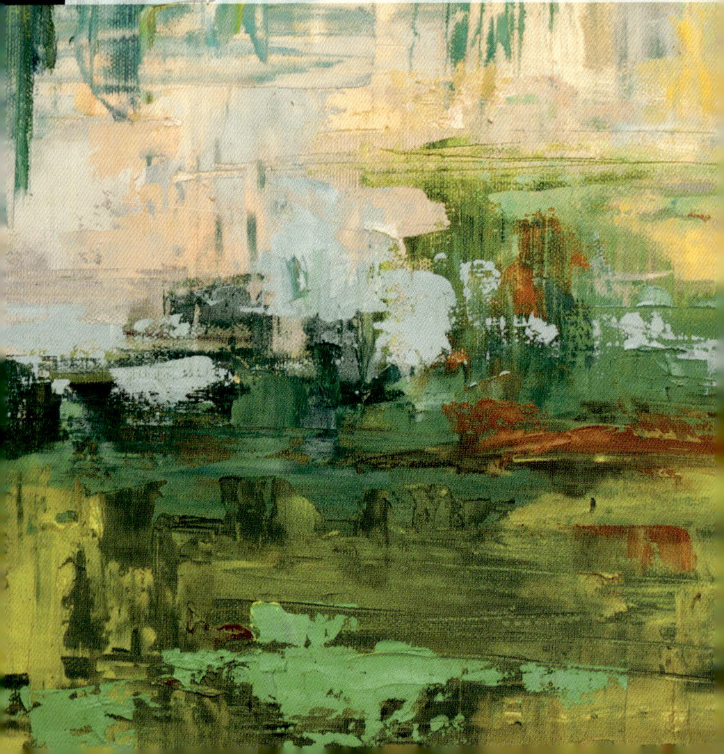

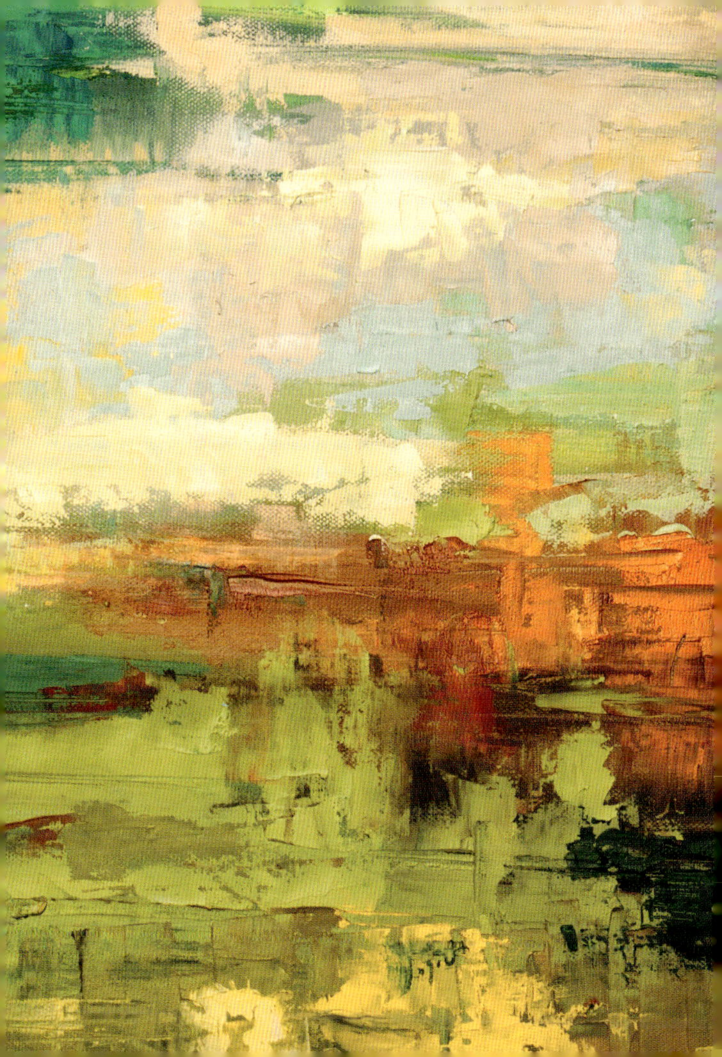

Learning to Use Your Tools

It's time to get familiar with the process of putting paint on the canvas. You may have the best colors and brushes, but until you learn how to control the flow of your paints and mediums, the entire painting process can feel random and frustrating. Here, we'll explore foundational brush techniques and provide straightforward exercises to help you build confidence and skill.

The Fat Over Lean Principle

This principle is a core concept in oil painting, key to layering color, and ensuring the longevity and structural integrity of your artwork.

To understand this principle, it's necessary to understand the basic structure of oil paints. Oil paints are, at their simplest, a combination of pigment (the color) and oil (typically linseed oil). The oil serves as the "vehicle," a means of controlling the distribution of pigment and binding it to the painting's surface. Over time, the oil dries and hardens, trapping the pigment in a durable film. This process is what gives oil paintings their characteristic richness, depth, and luminosity.

Oil painters learn to master the mechanics of oil itself, much like a watercolorist understands the properties of water. Paint directly from the tube typically has a thick, buttery consistency. While this is great for certain effects, its thickness means that a painter might only be able to make a few substantial brushstrokes before needing to reload.

To cover a larger area or achieve different consistencies, an artist needs to modulate the viscosity (flow) of the paint. This can be done in two main ways.

1. Adding a solvent: solvents (like mineral spirits or turpentine) thin the oil, reducing the paint's viscosity by breaking down the oil binder's structure. This makes the paint "leaner."

2. Adding more oil: this "fattens" the paint, making it flow more easily and increases the oil content relative to the pigment.

These two methods of modulating oil paint are where we get the terms "fat" and "lean," with fat paint containing a higher proportion of oil, and lean paint having been thinned with solvent, thus having a lower proportion of oil.

Here we see paint spread across a canvas surface. In the middle, the paint is unmodified. On the left, the same quantity of paint has been extended with a few drops of linseed oil. On the right, the same quantity of paint has been thinned with a few drops of odorless thinner.

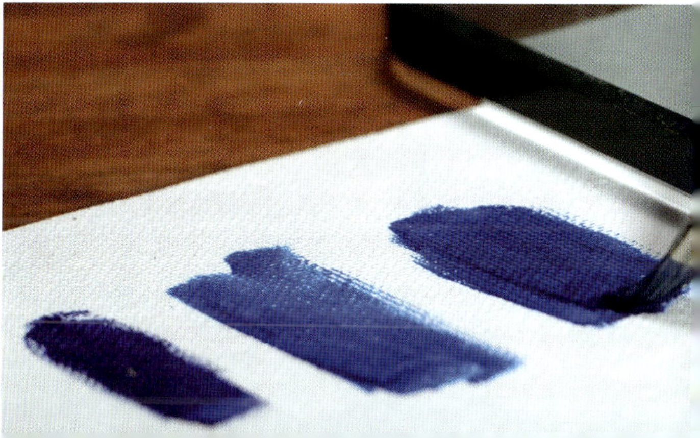

WHY IS THIS IMPORTANT?

Remember, the pigment in your paint is suspended within a layer of oil. The structural integrity of that oil film affects the longevity of your painting. Here's the key:

Lean layers (thinned with solvent) dry faster because the solvent evaporates quickly, leaving less oil to oxidize. As they dry, they also tend to shrink more.

Fat layers (with added oil) dry more slowly and remain flexible for a longer period.

If you apply a lean (fast-drying, more shrinking) layer over a fat (slow-drying, more flexible) layer, you're inviting trouble. The lean top layer will dry and shrink more rapidly than the still-flexible, oilier layer beneath it. This differential in drying and shrinking can cause the upper layer to crack and separate from the layer below, compromising your painting.

In this plein air study, details are being added with thicker, more oily paint on top of thinner, leaner layers of color.

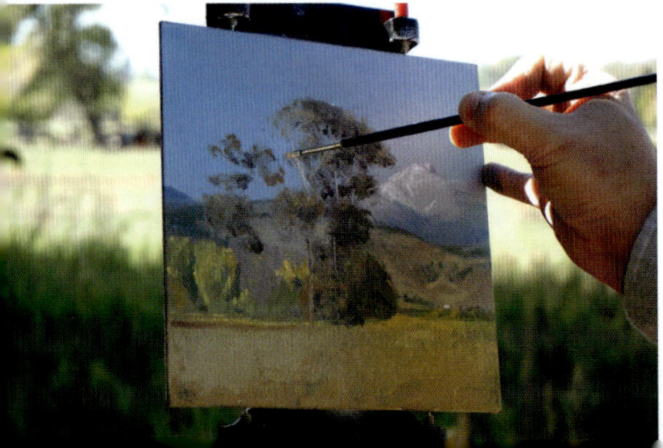

Artist Insight

The invention of pre-filled, collapsible tin paint tubes in 1841 was a game-changer for Impressionists. This allowed oil paint to be manufactured, stored for extended periods without drying out, and, most importantly, easily transported. Before this, oil paints were made in small batches by the artists themselves for each painting.

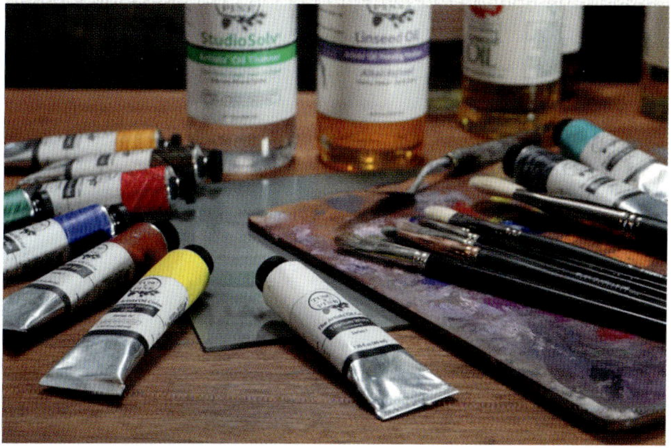

Fat Over Lean in Practice

Layering oil paints can be a frustrating process, often leading to muddy, overworked colors. Fortunately, the "fat over lean" principle is the key to avoiding this. Mastering this single concept will give you the confidence and control to build clean, vibrant layers every time. Let's explore how to put it into action.

INITIAL LAYERS

Start your painting with lean layers. This often means thinning your paint with a few drops of solvent (like mineral spirits or an odorless equivalent) for your initial drawing or when blocking in. These layers will dry relatively quickly and provide the painting with a stable base.

WET-IN-WET

This general rule can also help with layering color if you're working wet-in-wet (applying fresh paint into still-wet paint). If your initial "lean" layers are allowed some time to set up (become tacky but not fully dry), your subsequent, slightly "fatter" layers can be applied with less risk of excessively disturbing or muddying the underlayer.

SUBSEQUENT LAYERS

As you build up your painting, gradually reduce the amount of solvent you use and begin to incorporate more oil or a painting medium (which often contains oil, resin, and sometimes a bit of solvent). Each subsequent layer should be slightly "fatter" (containing more oil) or at least as fat as the layer beneath it.

Oil paint is a simple mixture of dry pigment and linseed oil.

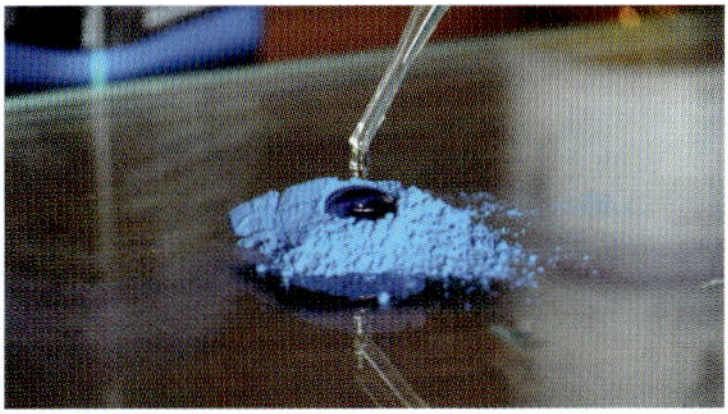

When ground together, oil and pigment mix together to create oil paint.

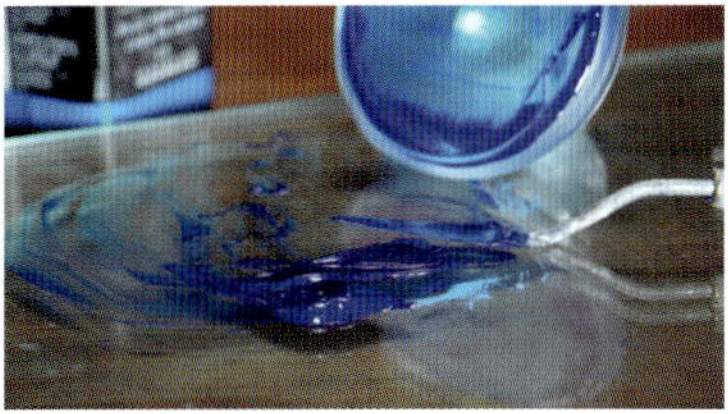

The flow of oil paint, or its viscosity, is affected by adding solvents and mediums. Here, we see paint made more fluid by adding linseed oil.

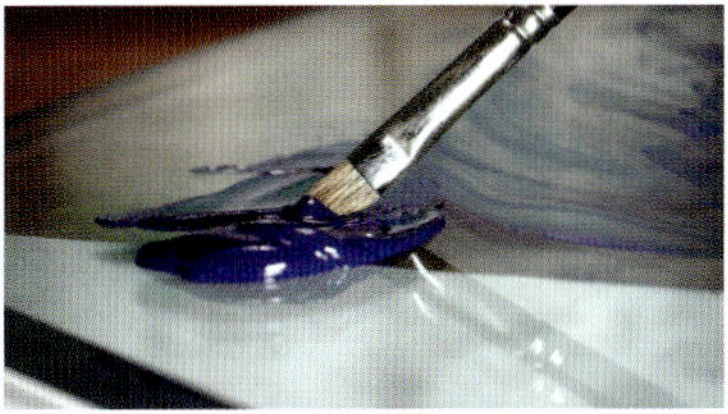

Paint can be layered following the "fat over lean" principle. Here, we see three layers of paint. The base layer is a "lean" paint thinned with solvent. Each additional layer contains less solvent and more linseed oil.

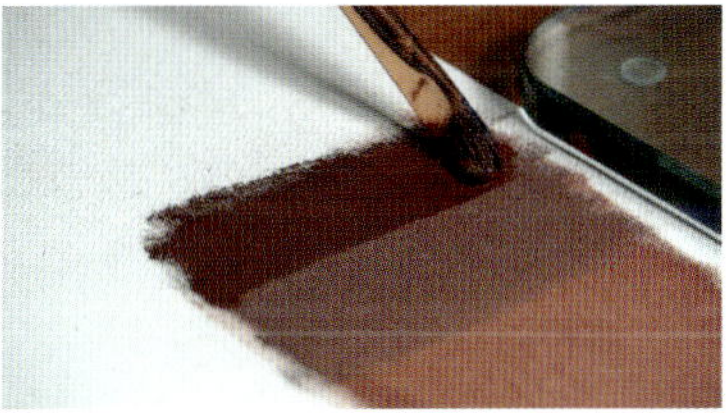

Direct Painting

With an understanding of how to manage your paint's consistency, let's start with making bold, confident marks on your canvas. Direct painting is all about applying paint with intention, creating marks that feel alive and spontaneous, rather than timidly dabbing. If you're drawn to paintings that feel dynamic and spontaneous, mastering confident brushstrokes is a great starting point.

FIVE STEPS FOR DIRECT PAINTING

1. Load your brush: don't be shy about loading your brush with a generous amount of paint. A well-loaded brush glides more smoothly and delivers a more assertive mark.

2. Adjust consistency: to cover larger areas or achieve a more fluid stroke for initial layers, you might thin your paint slightly with a solvent, creating a "leaner" mixture. To improve flow and brushing qualities, especially in later layers, you can add a painting medium or a small amount of oil (like linseed oil), making the paint "fatter." Always remember the "fat over lean" principle when doing so.

3. Engage your whole arm: try holding your brush a little more loosely, further up the handle. Think about moving your whole arm from the shoulder, not just wiggling your wrist. This promotes greater freedom and more fluid, expressive lines.

4. Vary the pressure: play around with how much pressure you apply. Pressing harder will generally give you thicker, bolder lines, while a lighter touch creates thinner, more delicate ones.

5. Commit to the stroke: the key is to commit to each mark you make. Don't hesitate! Apply the paint with decisiveness.

TRY THIS: LOADING PAINT

When loading the brush, keep the paint on the top half of the bristles. As paint works its way towards the handle and under the ferrule (the metal part that holds the bristles), it can be difficult to clean and lead to damage that may cause the bristles to swell and fall out over time.

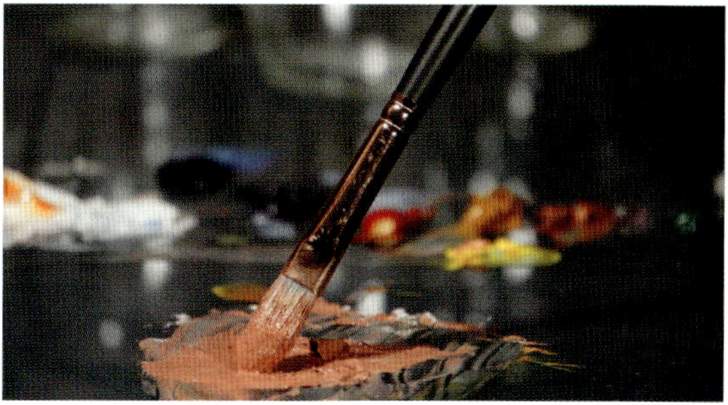

Blending

Sometimes you want colors to flow seamlessly into each other, like the soft gradations in a sunset or the gentle curve of a cheek. That's where blending comes in. It's all about creating smooth transitions between different colors. If you admire paintings with realistic forms, smooth surfaces, and soft transitions—think classical portraits or detailed still life paintings—blending techniques will become invaluable.

FIVE METHODS FOR BLENDING

1. Wet-in-wet blending: this is just what it sounds like—you blend colors together while they are both still wet on the canvas. Apply your colors next to each other, then use a clean, soft brush (like a mop brush, a soft filbert, or even a fan brush), or sometimes even your finger, to gently work the edges together. Work fairly quickly and with a light touch for the best results.

2. Stippling/tapping: you can lightly tap or stipple along the edges where colors meet using a stencil brush or a firm, dry brush. This can help soften the transition in a controlled way.

3. Dry blending (feathering): if your paint has started to dry a bit but is still workable, you can try dry blending. Use a clean, dry, soft brush and a very light, feathery touch to gently brush over the edges where the colors meet. This typically gives a softer, more subtle transition than wet-on-wet.

4. Optical blending: instead of physically mixing the paints on the canvas, you place small, distinct strokes of different colors right next to each other. When viewed from a normal distance, the eye mixes these colors together optically. This technique is a hallmark of Impressionism, creating vibrant, shimmering effects.

5. Glazing: this technique involves applying thin, transparent layers of color over an already dry layer of paint. You build up color and subtle gradations slowly, layer by layer. This can create incredible depth, luminosity, and nuanced transitions. Each glaze must be allowed to dry thoroughly before the next is applied. Remember "fat over lean:" glazes often involve more medium, making them "fatter," so they are suitable for later stages over leaner, dried underpaintings.

Wet-in-wet blending with a soft filbert brush.

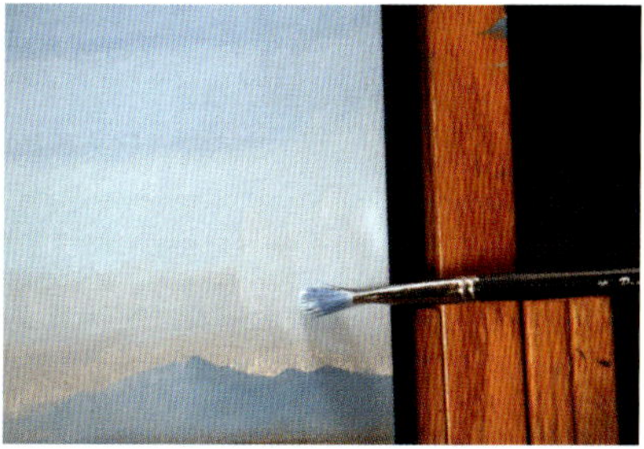

Create stipple blending by tapping with a stencil brush.

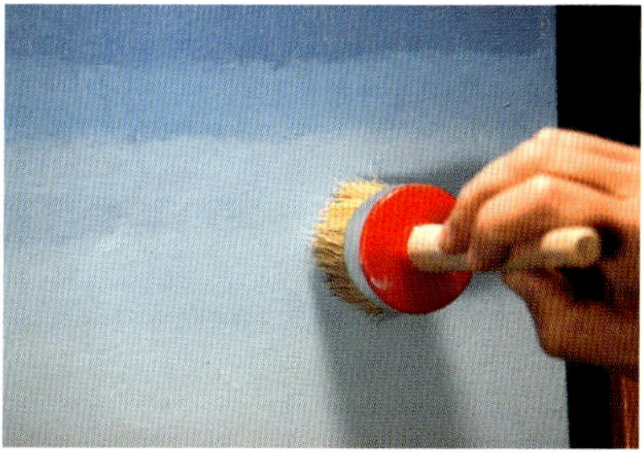

Feathering with a soft, dry mop brush to blend layers of wet paint.

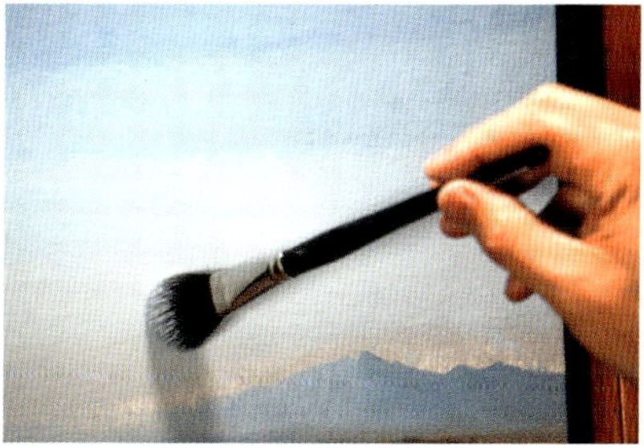

Creating Texture

Paint isn't just for creating smooth, flat surfaces! You can manipulate it to create a range of interesting textures that add dimension, visual interest, and excitement to your art.

FIVE METHODS FOR CREATING TEXTURE

1. Drybrush: this creates a broken, textured look, perfect for suggesting rough surfaces like tree bark, weathered stone, aged wood, or distant foliage. Use a brush with stiff bristles that is mostly dry, with very little paint on it. Drag or scuff the brush lightly across the canvas. The paint will catch on the raised texture of the canvas weave (or previous paint layers), leaving gaps and creating a scratchy, rough look.

2. Scumbling: for a softer, more atmospheric texture, try scumbling. This involves applying a thin layer of opaque or semi-opaque paint over a dry or tacky underlayer using a light, scrubbing, circular, or irregular dabbing motion. The underlying color shows through the gaps in the top layer, creating a lovely depth, subtle texture, and soft, broken edges. It's fantastic for creating misty or hazy effects, suggesting distant objects, building up soft foliage, or adding subtle layers of broken color.

3. Scraping: you can use a painting knife to scrape away areas of wet paint that you've already applied. This can reveal the color of the underlying layer or the canvas itself, creating interesting layered effects, sharp edges, and expressive marks. This is a favorite technique for artists who want a lot of texture, energy, and a sculptural quality.

4. Sgraffito: this is a fun and direct way to add lines and details by scratching into a wet layer of paint. Apply a layer of paint, and while it's still wet, use a tool like the handle of your brush, a palette knife tip, a sharpened stick, or a dedicated sgraffito tool to scratch lines or patterns into the paint. Timing is key. The paint needs to be wet enough to scratch into easily but not so wet that the lines immediately fill back in or blur. Sgraffito can create all sorts of cool linear details, like hair, fur, grass, intricate patterns, or calligraphic marks.

5. Impasto: if you enjoy working with thick, bold paint, you'll love palette knife techniques. Instead of brushes, you use palette knives or painting knives to apply thick dollops of paint ("impasto" means thick mixture in Italian) or to spread paint to create smooth, faceted areas.

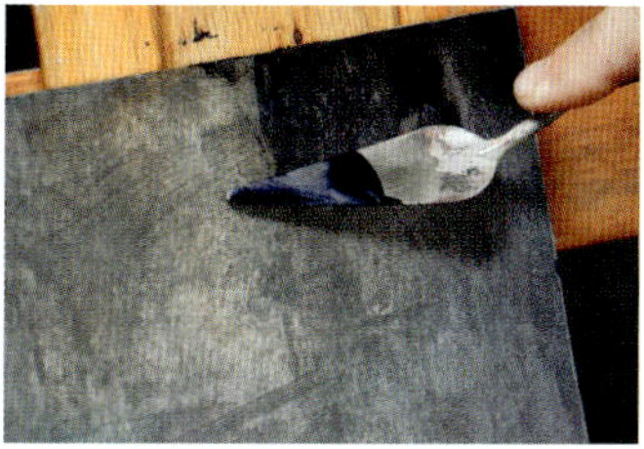

Scraping with a palette knife is useful for creating layered effects and textures.

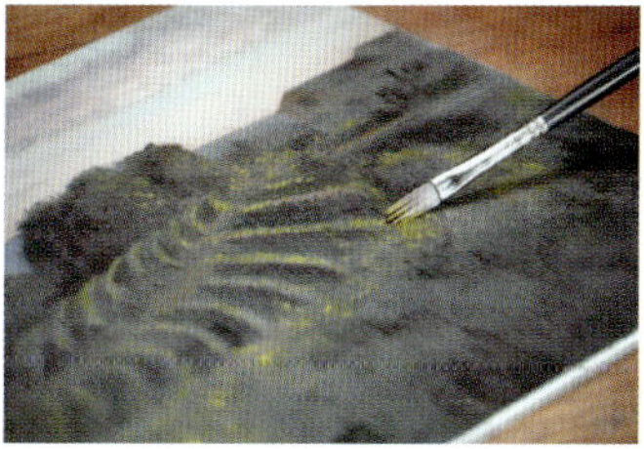

Here, a drybrush technique is used by lightly dragging a brush across the textured canvas to suggest the texture of leaves in this landscape.

TRY THIS: ADVANCED BRUSH CONTROL

To truly understand how your brushes behave with paint, dedicated practice is invaluable. These exercises will help you build finer control, dexterity, and confidence.

WASHES

This exercise focuses on applying thin, even layers of paint, used for underpaintings or creating smooth areas of color.

- Use a medium-sized filbert or flat brush, paint that's been thinned appropriately with medium or solvent, and a painting surface.
- To create a flat wash, load your brush with the thinned paint. Apply the color in broad, overlapping strokes, trying to achieve a consistent, even tone across an area without visible streaks or blotches. You might need to reload your brush consistently and work quite quickly.

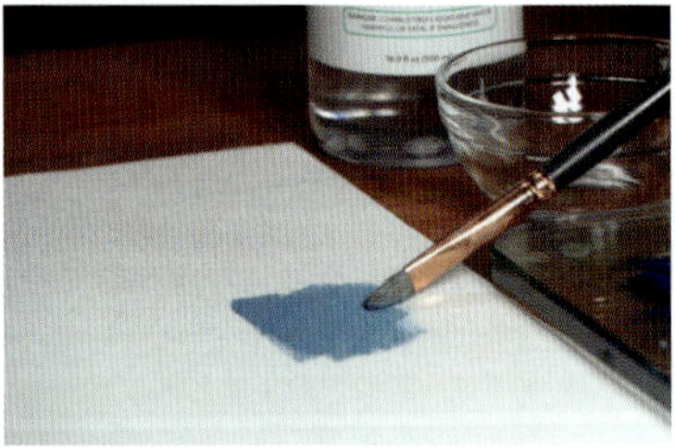

Practice washes to help create smooth, thin layers of color. This will be useful when creating initial thin layers of paint as well as glazes.

- To create a graded wash, start with a darker or more concentrated application of your thinned paint at one end of an area. As you work your way across or down, gradually add more medium/solvent to your brush (or less pigment) with each stroke, or progressively lighten pressure, so the color transitions smoothly from dark to light. Alternatively, you can blend two colors into a smooth gradient using a wash technique.
- To feather (or soften) the edge of a wash, you can use a clean, slightly damp or dry brush to gently feather the wet edge outwards with light, overlapping strokes. Wipe your brush frequently.

EXPERIMENT WITH BRUSHWORK

Remember, becoming comfortable and proficient with these brush techniques takes time, patience, and consistent practice. Don't be afraid to experiment, make "mistakes" (they are learning opportunities!), and try different approaches. The more you practice and play, the more you'll discover what feels natural and exciting for you.

CONTROLLED RELEASE

This exercise helps you understand how the angle of your brush and the amount of pressure you use dictate the amount of paint released and the resulting line width that is created.

- Use a large flat brush (1in/2.5cm is good for this) and some paint (not too thin, not too thick).
- Load your brush with paint. Hold the brush so the bristles are perpendicular to the surface, making a thin line.
- Begin to drag the brush across the surface. As you move, slowly lower the handle of the brush towards a more horizontal angle. Observe how the width of the paint mark increases as more of the flat side of the bristles comes into contact with the surface.
- Now start with the brush held more horizontally (creating a wide mark) and gradually raise the handle to a perpendicular position, narrowing the line.
- Try this with different brushes and vary the consistency of your paint to see how it affects the release of paint.

Controlled release exercises help with brush control. This will be useful for rendering form, expressive brushwork, and many finishing techniques.

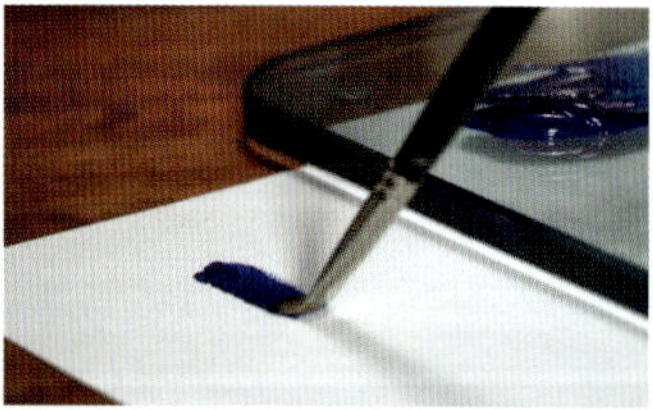

SHAPE FILLING

This exercise is all about precision and creating clean, well-defined shapes.

- Use a variety of brushes (rounds for detail, flats or filberts for larger areas), some paint, and a pencil.
- Lightly sketch some simple geometric shapes (squares, circles, triangles) and some more organic, irregular shapes on your surface.
- Practice filling these shapes with paint, aiming for perfectly crisp, clean edges. To better control the amount of paint at the edges, work from the inside of the shape towards the outline. Use a brush that is appropriate for the size of the shape or the section of the edge you are painting. For fine lines and sharp corners, a smaller round brush or the edge of a flat brush can be effective.
- Pay close attention to the angle you hold your brush and the consistency of your paint. Too thin, and it might bleed; too thick, and it might be hard to control the edge.

Shape filling exercises help to refine your skills with building layers, shapes, forms, and edges.

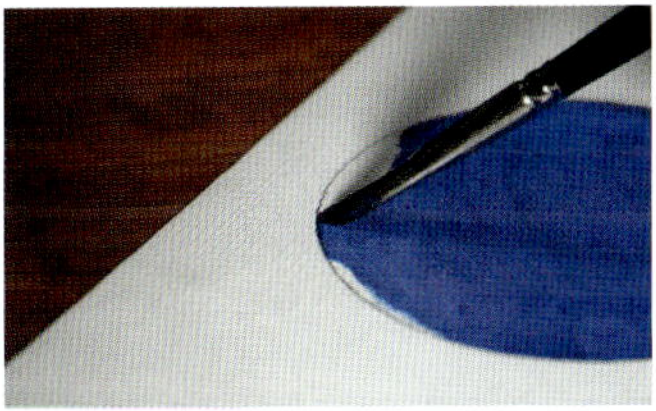

CHAPTER 5

Color Theory

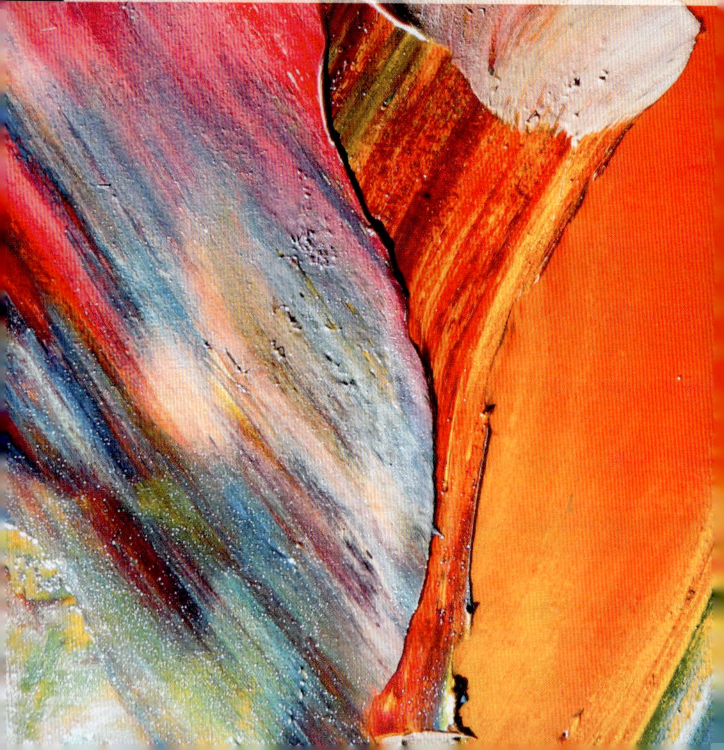

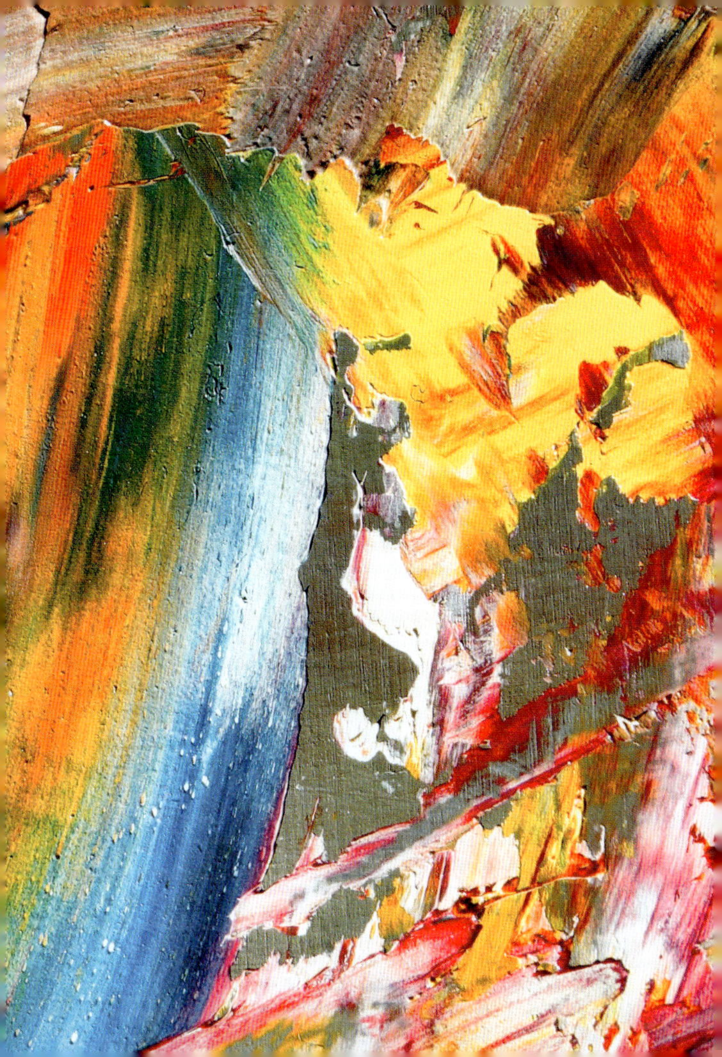

Exploring Color

Now it is time to look at color. Think of color not just as a decorative choice, but as the most powerful tool you have—a secret language for telling stories, creating space, and evoking emotion. To speak this language fluently, you must first understand its structure. This chapter is your guide to the fundamentals of color.

The Color Wheel

The color wheel is a guide to understanding the relationship between colors. Think of it as being built from the three primary colors: red, yellow, and blue. These are the foundational hues; they cannot be created by mixing other colors. From these primaries, the secondary colors are created: mixing red and yellow yields orange, blue and yellow yields green, and red and blue yields violet. Mixing a primary with a neighboring secondary creates tertiary colors: the nuanced, in-between colors like red-orange, yellow-green, and blue-violet that complete the spectrum.

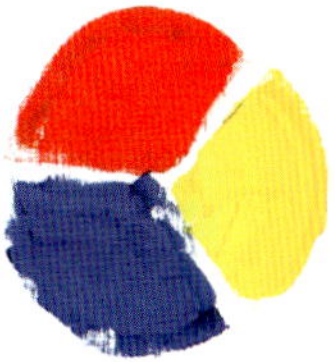

The color wheel is built from the three foundational primary colors of red, yellow, and blue.

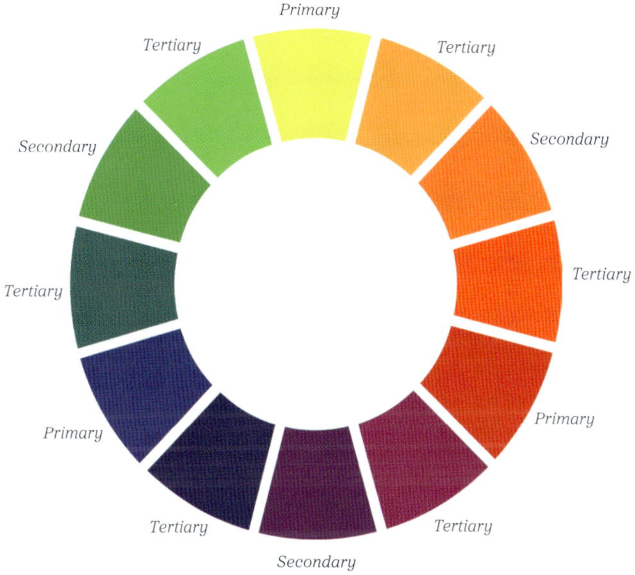

COLOR SCHEMES

The color wheel helps us understand the relationships between colors and how to put them together.

Complementary colors are those directly opposite each other on the wheel (red and green, blue and orange, yellow and violet). This opposition creates a powerful dynamic. Placed side-by-side, they intensify one another, creating a vibrant visual contrast that makes each color appear brighter. However, when mixed, they neutralize each other, creating complex browns, grays, and muted tones essential for realistic shadows and earthy palettes.

This study of a sunrise is based on a complementary palette of orange and blue. This is not a strict complementary painting, however, as there are subtle variations in hue, value, and saturation in both the sky and ground areas.

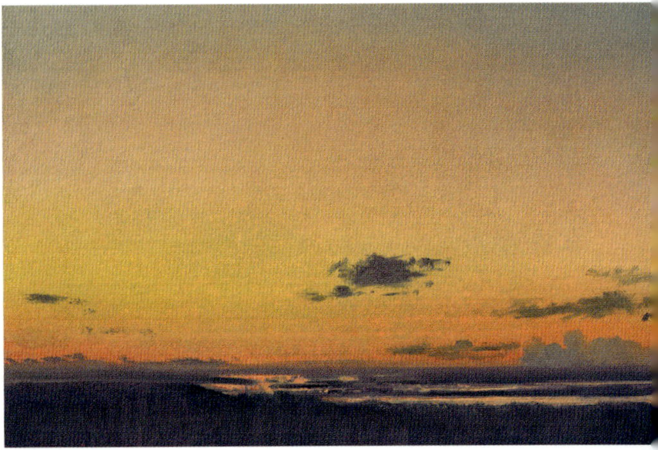

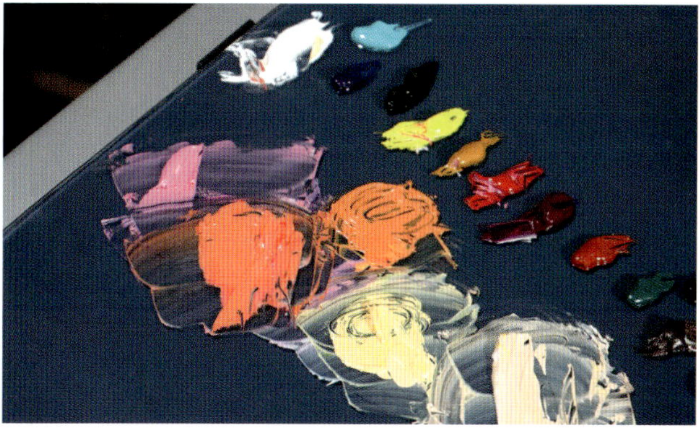

Here are analogous colors mixed for use in the sunrise painting opposite. Once I had determined that the base for the sky color would be orange, I created some variety by expanding the sky colors into a set of yellow, orange, and red, all of which are adjacent to one another on the color wheel.

Analogous colors are neighbors on the wheel, typically in a group of three to five. Using these color families (like yellow, yellow-orange, and orange) is the key to creating effortless harmony and a calm, unified mood in your work.

Neutrals—black, white, and grays—are the essential anchors of your palette. They are your primary tools for controlling a color's lightness and darkness.

Hue, Value, and Saturation

Every color you will ever mix can be defined and controlled by just three properties. Understanding these is the key to making intentional, powerful color choices.

Hue is a color's fundamental identity and name (red, blue, green). Being able to confidently identify the core hue of every paint on your palette is the first step.

Value describes how light or dark a color is on a scale from pure white to pure black.

Saturation is the purity, intensity, or vividness of a color. Think of saturation (also known as chroma) as the volume control for your color. A highly saturated color is loud, bright, and energetic. A less saturated color is quieter and more subtle.

To familiarize yourself with these concepts, engage with your materials directly.

- First, lay out your paint tubes and identify the core hue of each one.
- Next, using a gray scale and value finder (available online and at most art supply stores), place each tube next to it to determine its approximate value. This simple act builds instant recognition.
- Now, let's explore saturation. Choose one vibrant hue, like red. Paint a swatch of the pure color. Then, create a gray mixture using black and white paint. Mix in a tiny bit of gray and paint another swatch beside it. Continue adding small amounts of gray, creating a scale that moves from highly saturated to completely muted. This exercise makes the concept of saturation much more tangible.

Identify the hue of your paint with the help of a color wheel.

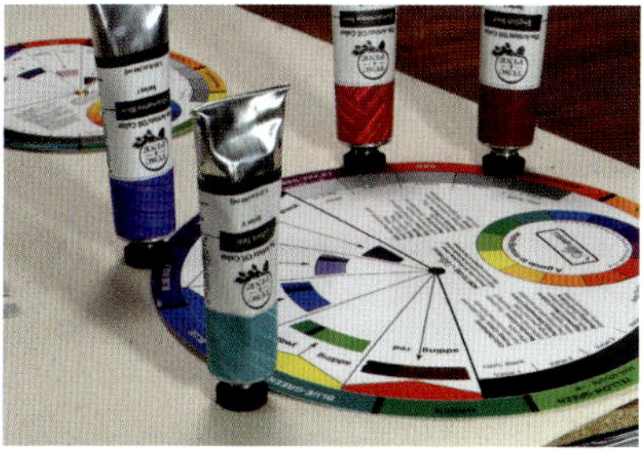

Identify the value of your paint using a gray scale and value finder to determine how light or dark it is.

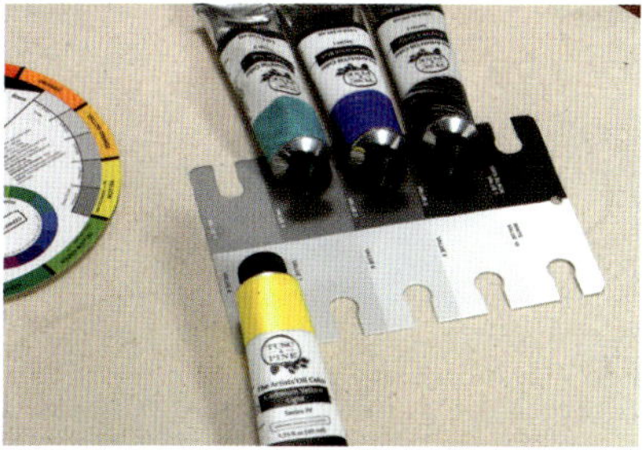

Explore saturation in action by adding progressively more gray to a single hue.

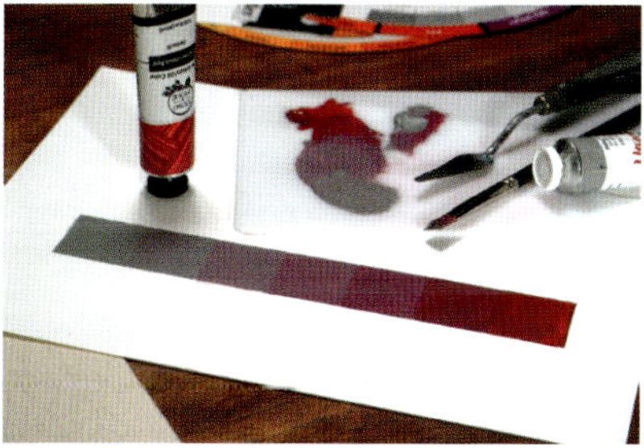

Temperature

Along with the three properties of hue, value, and saturation, color also has a "temperature" that directly affects the mood of your painting and your ability to create depth.

Warm colors (reds, oranges, yellows) are associated with sunlight and fire. They feel energetic and tend to advance, making objects feel closer to the viewer.

Cool colors (blues, greens, violets) are associated with water and shade. They feel calm and tend to recede, creating a sense of distance and serenity.

Recognizing the subtle temperature bias in your paints is a mixing superpower. Even within a single hue, there are warm and cool versions. For example, Ultramarine Blue has a red bias, making it a warm blue, while Phthalo Blue has a green bias, making it a cool blue. Understanding this allows you to mix cleaner, more intentional colors.

One of the most powerful applications of temperature is creating depth through atmospheric perspective. In nature, distant objects appear cooler and less saturated due to the atmosphere. You can replicate this by using warmer, more intense colors for objects in the foreground and progressively cooler, more muted colors for objects in the background. This is a highly effective way to make a flat canvas feel like a vast, three-dimensional space.

The depth and atmosphere in this landscape is created through the strategic use of warm and cool colors. Cool colors (blues, grays, and pale violets) are used in the sky and distant mountains, while warm colors (deep orange and yellow) are used in the foreground.

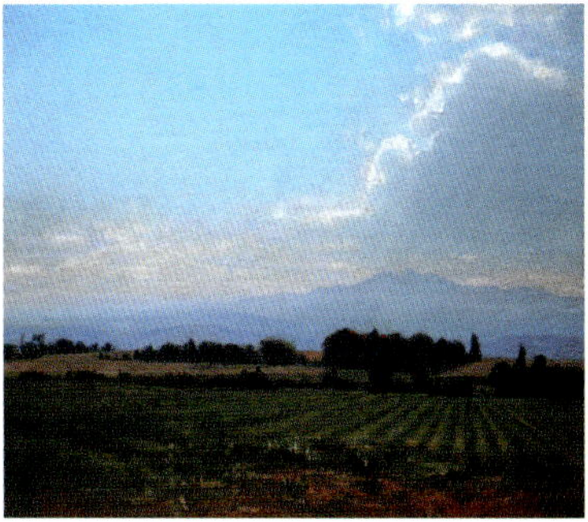

TRY THIS: WARM AND COOL COLOR MIXING

Let's see the difference between warm and cool colors in your own paints. Find your warmest red (like Cadmium Red Light) and your coolest red (like Quinacridone Magenta). Mix a little white into each of them separately to make lighter versions (tints). Look at the tints side-by-side. See how the warm red tint still feels very "red" and vibrant, while the cool red tint might look a little more pink or even slightly violet? Repeat this exercise with a warm yellow (like Cadmium Yellow Deep) and a cool yellow (like Cadmium Yellow Light), and then with a warm blue (like Ultramarine Blue) and a cool blue (like Phthalo Blue). Paying attention to these subtle temperature differences will make a big difference in your mixing.

Artist Insight

Georges Seurat wanted to elevate painting into a science. Drawing on theorists like Michel-Eugène Chevreul, Seurat applied distinct strokes of color to force the viewer's eye into optical mixing. His systematic method exploited contrast to achieve the "maximum luminosity scientifically possible," as he explored the idea that harmony and emotional expression could be described as a set of scientific laws.

"La rade de Grandcamp," Georges Seurat, 1885, oil on canvas, private collection.

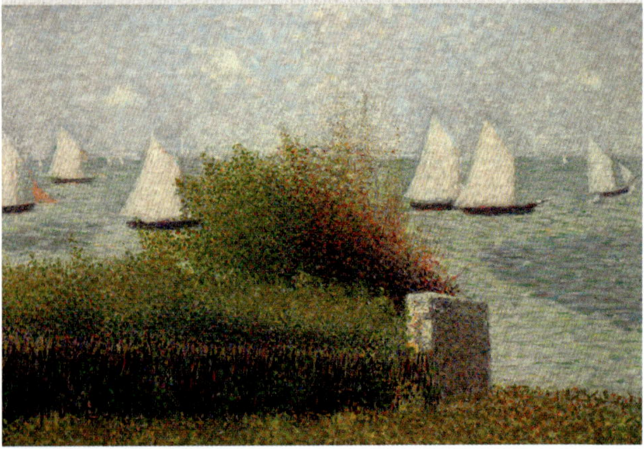

Embrace the Colorful Adventure!

Remember, mastering color is an exciting, ongoing adventure. Keep experimenting, keep mixing, and keep exploring! The more you work with color, the more intuitive it will become, and the more confidently you'll be able to use it to create the paintings you envision.

This painting demonstrates how control of hue, value, and saturation creates a convincing suggestion of light and depth. Notice how distant features are painted with colors that are lower in saturation, while in the foreground, colors are warmer and there is greater value contrast.

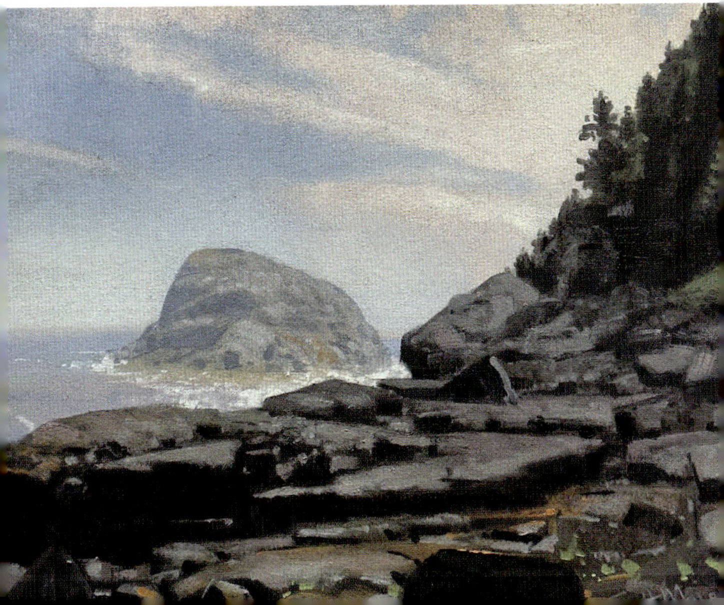

CHAPTER 6

Color Mixing

Creating Colors

This chapter is all about the nitty-gritty of mixing paint! Forget just squeezing color onto your brush, we're going to learn how to create the exact colors you want, empowering you to make intentional color choices. This chapter will equip you with an understanding of color relationships, allowing you to build a palette that is your own, giving you the freedom to make every mark count.

Setting Up Your Palette

Keeping an organized palette makes your mixing faster, more efficient, and less frustrating. A logical setup means you can find the colors you need quickly and keeps your mixing space nice and clean.

Over time, you will develop a sequence of colors that works best for you. A common and helpful layout is to start with your white paint in the top left corner, followed by blues, yellows, reds, earth tones, and ending with black.

I arrange my own palette with white on the left, followed by warm and cool blues, yellows, earth tones, reds, and ending with black. Other artists might arrange their palettes with warm colors on one side and cool on the other. Leave a large empty space in the middle of your palette as your dedicated mixing zone.

Don't be shy with your paint! Squeeze out a good amount of each color you think you'll need for your painting session. It's always better to have a little extra than not enough.

Once you determine the layout of colors on your palette, there is a distinct advantage to maintaining that specific order every time you paint. Whether you arrange pigments from warm to cool or light to dark, this consistency helps build muscle memory. Over time, your hand will learn to find the right color instinctively, eliminating the need to pause and search for a specific tube. By removing this friction, the mixing process becomes smoother and more intuitive.

This is an example of a palette that I use, starting with white and moving from blues to yellow and reds to black.

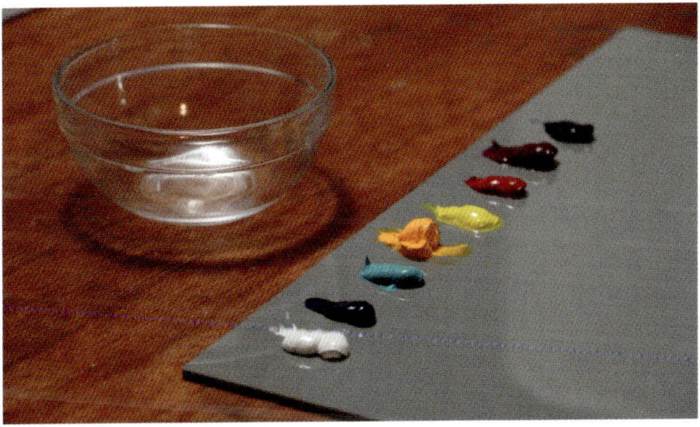

Mixing Techniques

Trying to mix every color imaginable right away can be overwhelming, so start by mixing with a limited palette. This means working with just a few key colors, usually a warm and cool version of each primary (red, yellow, blue) plus white. This encourages you to learn how colors combine and deepens your understanding of color relationships.

While brushes are for painting, your palette knife is for mixing. It's the best tool for getting paint thoroughly and evenly mixed without wasting paint or muddying your colors. Using a knife also keeps your brushes cleaner for applying paint to your canvas.

Wiping your palette knife clean between colors helps to avoid mixing muddy colors. Sometimes, however, mixing with a dirty palette knife can help you discover new and unique neutral colors, so don't be afraid to try.

When you're mixing, start with the lighter color in your mixture and gradually add the darker color. It's easier to slowly make a light color darker than to try and make a dark color lighter (which often requires more white and can make the color look chalky).

A simple, limited palette can be built from warm and cool versions of the three primary colors. Here we see a comparison of the primary colors with warm versions on top and cool on bottom.

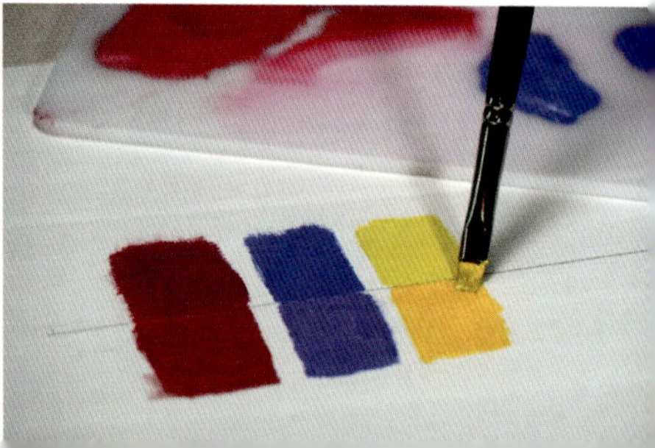

MIXING DARK INTO LIGHT

1. Put a small dollop of your lighter color (like white or yellow) in your mixing area. Clean your palette knife. Now, pick up just a tiny amount of the darker color on the very tip of your knife.

2. Gently fold and press that darker color into the lighter one using your knife, mixing it thoroughly until the color is even.

3. Look at the result. Need it darker? Pick up another tiny bit of the darker color and mix again. Be patient! It's always easier to add more dark paint than to try and take it away.

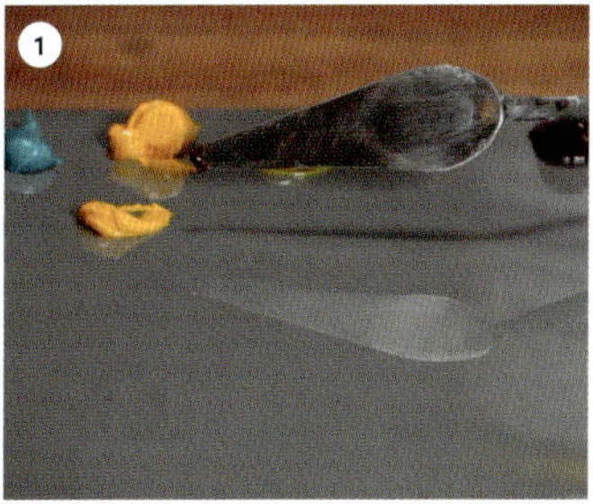

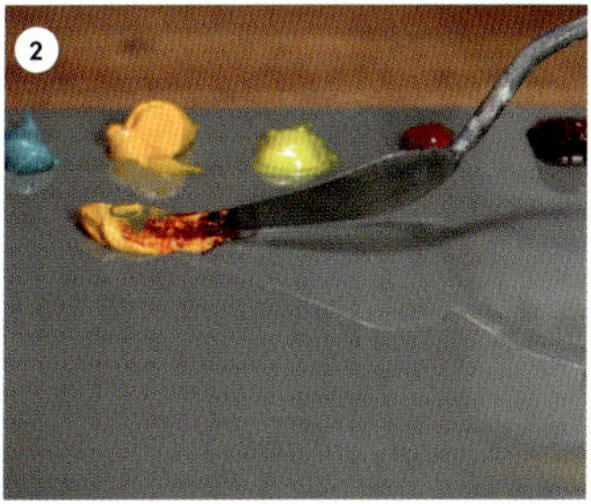

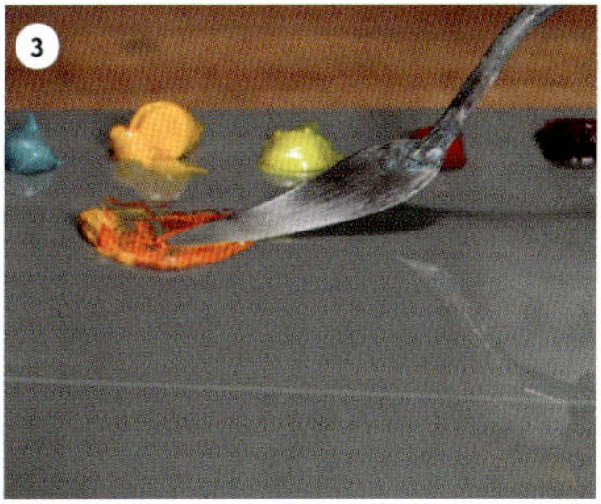

Think back to the warm and cool temperature biases we touch upon in the previous chapter. Those biases are key when you're mixing! Knowing that Ultramarine Blue leans slightly towards violet (making it warmer) or that Phthalo Blue leans towards green (making it cooler) helps you predict what kind of color you'll get when you mix them with other paints.

For example, if you want a more vibrant green, you'll get a cleaner, brighter result by mixing a cool yellow with a cool blue, rather than using warmer versions that might give you a duller, muddier green.

A brighter green (right) is created by mixing cool blue and cool yellow, compared to a dull, warm green (left) mixed using warm yellow and blue.

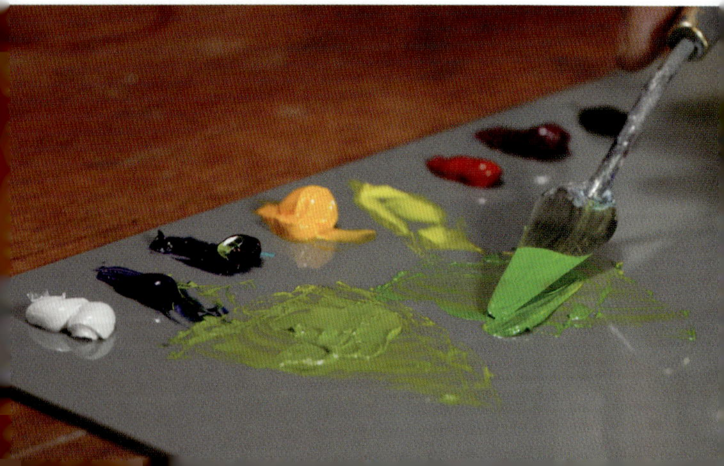

Keep your color wheel nearby as you mix. It's a quick visual reminder of how colors relate. Use it to help you figure out which colors to mix to get a specific hue, to understand why certain combinations create vibrant or muted colors, and to predict the outcome of your mixtures based on where the colors sit on the wheel.

The best way to get good at color mixing is to simply experiment and practice! Don't be afraid to mix different colors together just to see what happens. Observe the results and learn from them. Every mix is a learning opportunity.

Experiment with color mixing, like this example, where mixing a small amount of Ultramarine Blue into an orange mixture will create a warm, neutral green.

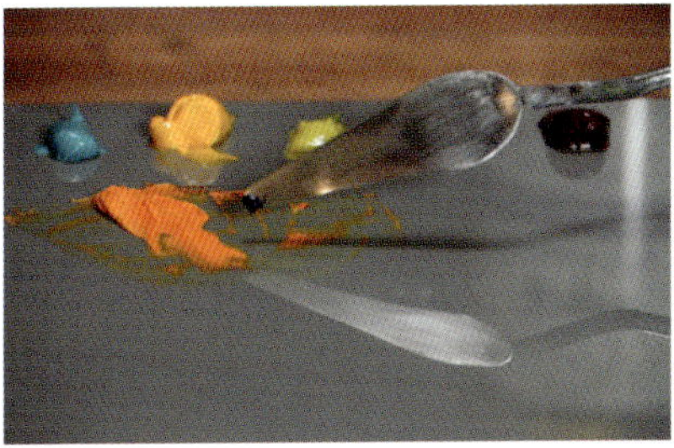

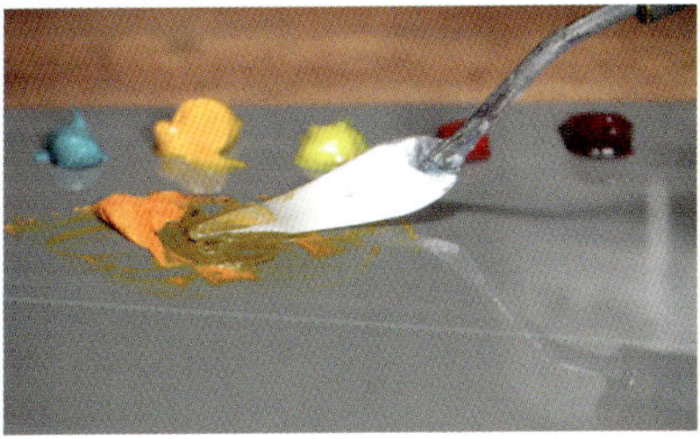

TRY THIS: CREATE A COLOR MIXING CHART

Making color charts is an excellent way to become more familiar with your paints. Begin by creating a simple grid that documents combinations of the paints in your current palette. But more importantly, use space to document any unique mixtures you discover—those perfect, personal colors you create by experimenting. And when you add a new color to your collection, make a chart specifically to see how it mixes with your existing colors. These charts become invaluable tools, showing you the unique quality of each pigment and helping you refine your palette.

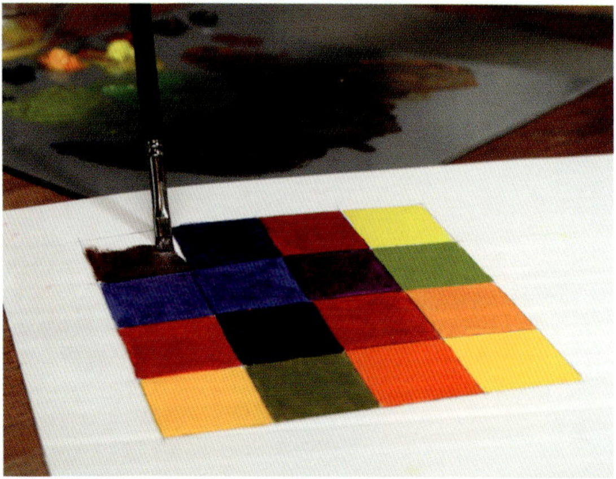

Expanding Your Palette

While understanding the principles is key, having some starting points or "recipes" for common colors can be helpful as you begin. Different paint brands and even different batches of the same pigment can vary, so always observe your mix and adjust as needed.

- **For a rich, nuanced black** that has more life than black straight from the tube, try mixing Ultramarine Blue and Burnt Sienna (creates a slightly cool black) or Alizarin Crimson and Phthalo Green (creates a more neutral black).
- **For vibrant greens,** combine a cool yellow (like Lemon Yellow) with a cool blue (like Phthalo Blue). Adjust the amounts to get bluer or yellower greens. For more muted greens, start with your vibrant green mix and add a tiny touch of its complement (red) or an earth tone like Yellow Ochre or Raw Umber.
- **For soft, natural neutral greens** often seen in landscapes, start with a slightly muted green base by mixing a cool yellow and a warm blue. Then, add earth tones like Yellow Ochre, Raw Umber, or Burnt Sienna to make them even softer and more natural-looking.

Keep experimenting to discover new "recipes" to expand your palette. This combination of Ultramarine Blue and Burnt Sienna creates a rich, dark color that can be used instead of black from the tube.

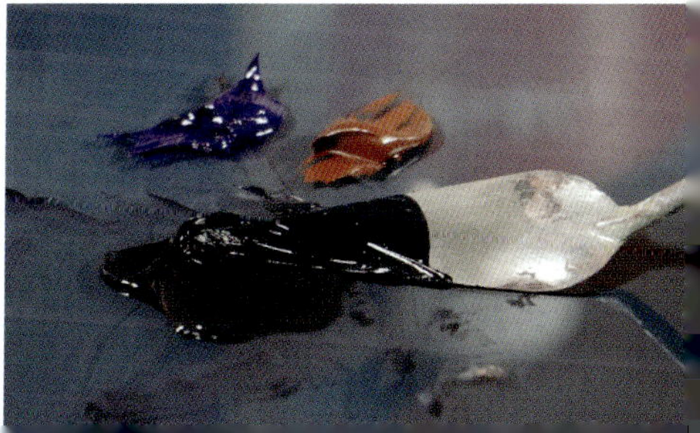

- **For bright, warm oranges,** mix a warm red (like Cadmium Red Light) with a warm yellow (like Cadmium Yellow Deep). Play with the ratios to get red-oranges or yellow-oranges.
- **For beautiful, deep violets,** a classic mix is warm blue (like Ultramarine Blue) and cool red (like Alizarin Crimson). Adjust the amounts to get bluer or redder violets.
- **Versatile browns** can be mixed in a number of ways. Mixing any complementary pair will produce a brown. Try blue + orange or red + green. Start with the cooler color and slowly add the warmer one until you get a brown tone. You can also mix browns by combining red, yellow, and blue in different proportions. Experiment to find redder, yellower, or cooler browns.
- **Mixing skin tones** is all about observing and adjusting. A good starting point for a medium skin tone is Yellow Ochre, Cadmium Red Light, and a touch of Raw Sienna. Lighten it with white for lighter skin tones. To darken, use a tiny touch of Burnt Umber, Ultramarine Blue, or a very small amount of black (too much black can make skin tones look flat).

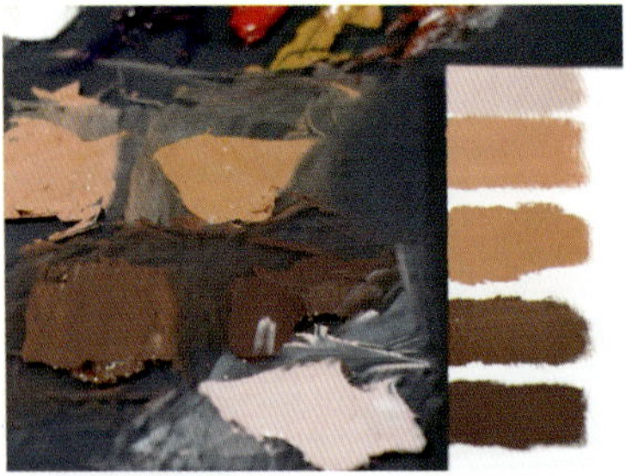

Before tackling a portrait, practice mixing a range of tones to become familiar with the ratios needed to achieve the color of skin.

Correcting Color Mistakes

Learning how to correct mistakes and adjust your colors as you're mixing is one of the most important skills to develop. First, identify the direction the color needs to shift. Is the color too light or too dark (value issue)? Is it too bright or too dull (saturation issue)? Or is it leaning towards the wrong color entirely (hue issue)?

- **Value issue:** if it's too light, add a tiny bit of a darker color from your palette or a touch of its complement. Avoid black unless you want a very specific effect. If it's too dark, add a small amount of white or a lighter version of that color.
- **Saturation issue:** if the color is too bright, add a tiny amount of its complementary color (a little red will tone down a bright green, for example) or mix in a neutral gray. If it's too dull, add a small amount of a more saturated version of that color (you might need to mix a purer, brighter version and add it).
- **Hue issue:** if your color is leaning the wrong way (like your green is too yellow), use your color wheel! Add a tiny bit of the color that is opposite the unwanted hue on the wheel. If your green is too yellow, a little bit of red-violet (which is opposite yellow-green) will nudge it back towards a truer green.

Sometimes a mix just goes wrong. It becomes muddy, overworked, or you just can't seem to get it right. It's perfectly okay to scrape it off your palette or even your canvas and start fresh. However, if you have the patience to work with muddy colors and appreciate them as learning moments, you'll ultimately develop a deeper, more nuanced appreciation for color.

Color Study Walk-Through

The best way to learn how to mix paint is to put it into action. For this example, I chose to paint a quick color study of a single tomato, with the objective of mixing the average color of the light side, shadow, and highlight. As a color mixing exercise, I'm less concerned with painting details and correcting proportions.

Throughout the process, I use strips of paper on which I can paint swatches of color. Holding these painted samples up to the subject allows me to better understand the changes I need to make in order to arrive at the correct color.

THE BASE HUE

My first objective is to identify the base hue to serve as a foundation for the average color of the lit portion of the tomato. I have three different red paints on my palette: Cadmium Red (warm red on the bottom swatch), Venetian Red (an earthy red in the middle), and Quinacridone Magenta (a cool red on top). Comparing these samples, I determine that the base red is closest to Cadmium Red, but shifts towards the Venetian Red as well.

CORRECTING THE LIGHT SIDE HUE

With the base hue determined, the hue can be refined further. The first step is to create a mixture of Cadmium Red and Venetian Red (top swatch). This swatch is held up against the subject. This resulting color appears close, but a little dark. The lit portion of the tomato also appears slightly more orange than the swatch. The color is then mixed further, adding small amounts of Cadmium Yellow until I'm more confident in the color match (bottom swatch). In this case, the value seems correct as well, so I don't need to make it lighter or darker.

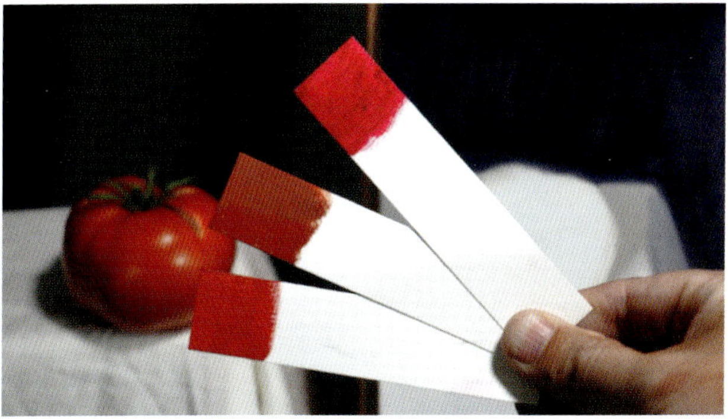

The base hue—comparing three colors against the subject to determine the base color.

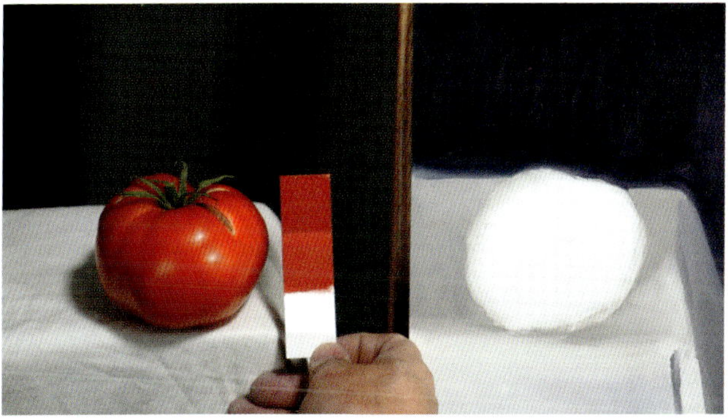

Correcting the light side—adjusting the color further with color swatches helps to identify the decisions needed to make a stronger color match.

CORRECTING THE SHADOW SIDE HUE

I block in the average color for the light side. Then, it's time to discover the average color for the shaded areas of the tomato. My first step is to simply mix Payne's Gray (a dark, neutral gray hue) into the color mixed for the light side. With the average color for the light side painted as a swatch to serve as a comparison (top swatch), this initial shadow color is added (second swatch). We can immediately see that it is too dark and the saturation has been reduced too much. Adding a small amount of white, the color is lightened in value, but now it becomes too light in value and the color is too neutral (third swatch). To arrive at the correct color, I experiment by adding more Cadmium Red and a small amount of Cadmium Yellow to increase the saturation. Adding a tiny amount of Ultramarine Blue lowers the value and makes the color cooler, and we arrive at a color that is closer to the average shadow color (bottom swatch).

COMPLETING THE STUDY

The shadow areas are brushed in, and the highlight colors are established. The highlight color is a simple pink-ish mixture of Titanium White and Cadmium Red. However, if we allow ourselves to be too concerned with details, refinement, correcting proportions, and other painting issues, we may become less attuned to color. It's important to remember that color studies like this are best painted as rough sketches, sacrificing details and refinement for a focus on color.

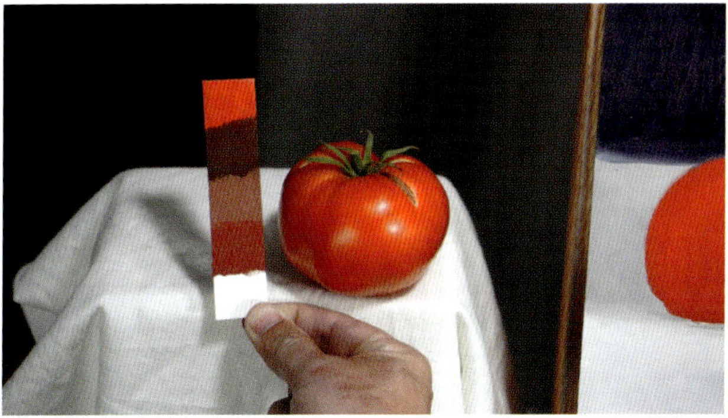

Correcting the shadow side–painting shadows is not a matter of simply adding black and red together. It's a nuanced adjustment process.

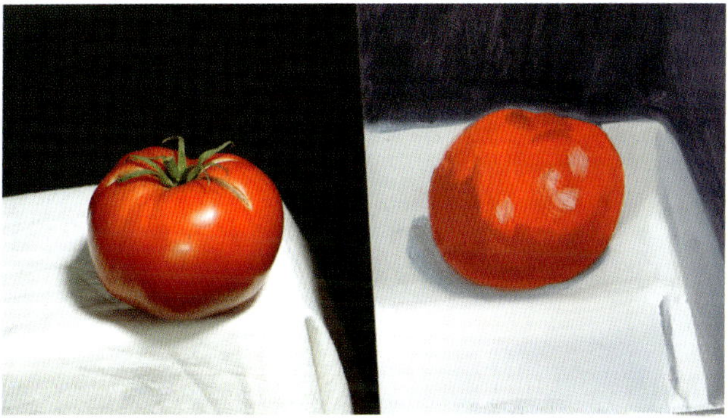

Completing the study–when creating a color study, sacrifice details and refinement to focus entirely on capturing the essence of color.

TRY THIS: COLOR CAMOUFLAGE

Here's a challenge that requires patience, observation, and a methodical approach, but will help you master your color mixing skills.

Gather a selection of small color samples. These could be cut from magazines, snippets of fabric, or small objects from around the house. Your challenge is to mix a color that precisely matches each of your samples. Begin by observing your sample and matching its base hue. Once the hue is a perfect match, move onto adjusting the saturation. If the sample is duller than your mix, slowly add a small amount of its complementary color until the intensity is correct. Finally, adjust the value (lightness or darkness) until it matches your sample perfectly. For best results, use a complement to darken your mix and a lighter version of the color to lighten it. This three-step process—hue, saturation, value—will help you develop the skills to match any color you encounter with expert precision.

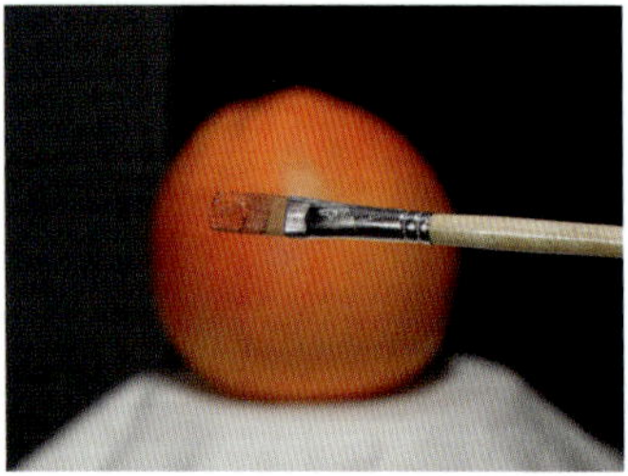

Practice precise color mixing by matching your paint to simple objects. Start by correcting its hue first, then its saturation (using complements), and finally its value.

Artist Insight

Wassily Kandinsky, a trailblazer of abstract art, had a rare condition called synesthesia, which meant he experienced colors as sounds and music. This deeply influenced his ideas that specific colors could stir emotions and had spiritual meaning, often linking them to certain shapes—like energetic yellow with a triangle, or peaceful blue with a circle. In his important 1911 book, *Concerning the Spiritual in Art*, Kandinsky argued that art could powerfully affect the human spirit directly through color and form, without needing to show recognizable objects.

"Improvisation Klamm," Wassily Kandinsky, 1914, oil on canvas, Lenbachhaus, Munich.

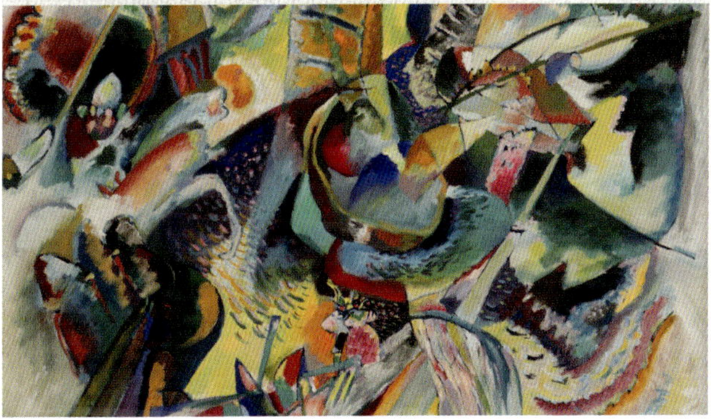

CHAPTER 7

Understanding Composition

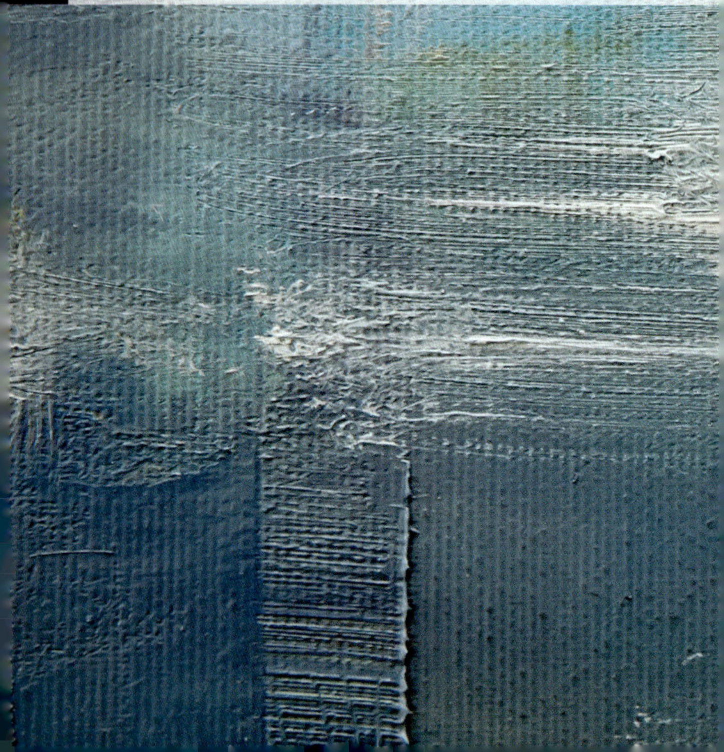

Arranging Your Artwork

Composition is the art of deciding where everything goes, how it all fits together, and how you guide the viewer's eye through your work. It's about making intentional choices to create something balanced, engaging, and meaningful. It's not about following rigid rules, it's about using some incredibly helpful guidelines to make your paintings stronger.

The Elements of Composition

Before we talk about arranging things, let's get familiar with the basic stuff you'll be arranging! Think of these as the building blocks, your visual vocabulary.

Lines aren't just outlines. They can be actual lines you paint or even imaginary lines created by the way objects are placed or the direction of brushstrokes. They lead the viewer's eye through your painting, creating a sense of movement, and connecting different parts of your composition. Use them to lead the eye right to your area of focus.

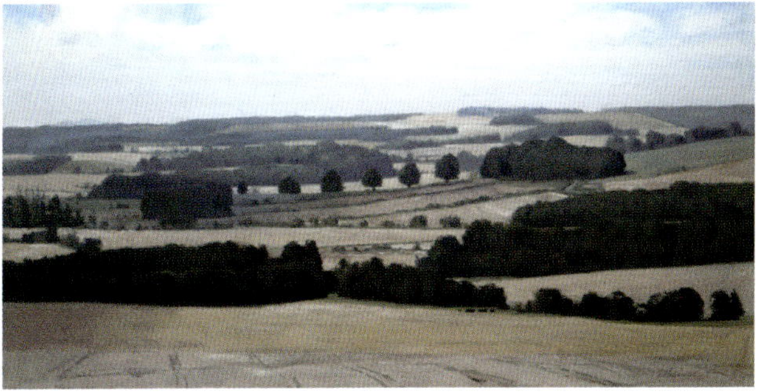

In "Road to Alnwick," the trees and hedges provide natural lines to paint, leading the eye across the width of the painting.

Here, in "Lindisfarne, Sunrise," notice how the stone wall creates a line that zigzags through the composition towards the sharp, silhouetted line of the hill and the focal point of the castle.

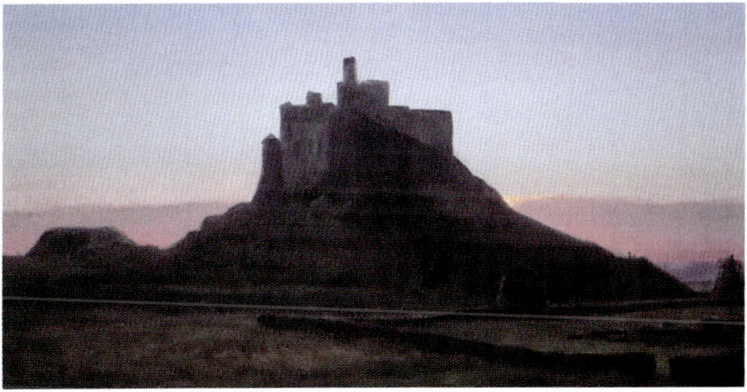

Edges are where one thing meets another, where forms are defined. The quality of an edge becomes a powerful tool in composition. Sharp, crisp edges make things look close and precise. Soft, blurry edges recede and create a sense of atmosphere. And sometimes, letting an edge just fade or blend away (lost edges) can add mystery and make a form feel more integrated into its surroundings. Playing with different edge types will add depth and visual interest to your painting.

"Leptis Magna" features a variety of edges, including hard (A), soft (B), and lost (C) edges. This helps to create a sense of atmosphere and light.

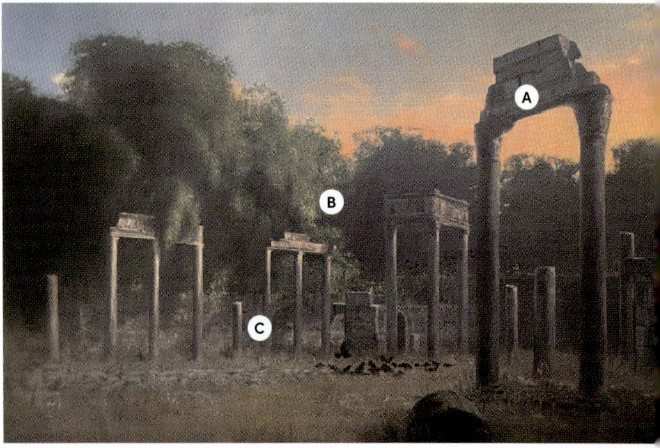

Artist Insight

Paul Cézanne, who some consider the father of modern art, had a profound influence on modern abstraction. His approach revolutionized painting through his emphasis on nature's underlying geometric forms—cylinders, spheres, and cones—and his use of "constructive brushstrokes" to describe objects with patches of color. Cézanne deliberately played with classical perspective, painting multiple viewpoints and prioritizing the structural integrity of the composition.

"Mount Sainte-Victoire," Paul Cézanne, c. 1904, oil on fabric, The Cleveland Museum of Art, Cleveland.

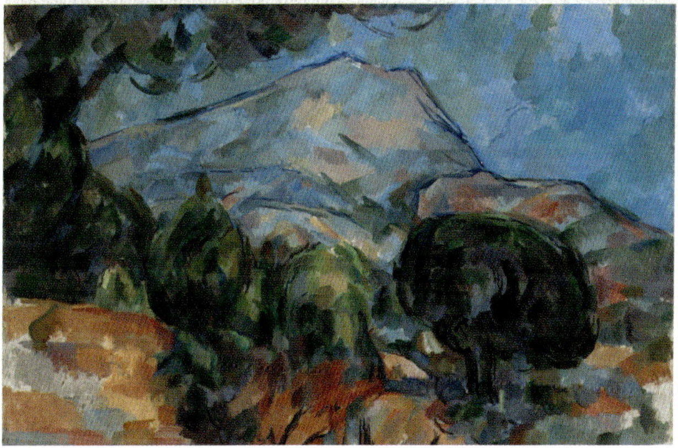

Shapes are the fundamental forms in your painting, or your building blocks. Think about the big shapes: are they structured and geometric (like squares and circles) or more natural and flowing (organic shapes)? Also, remember that the empty spaces around your objects are also shapes (negative shapes), and they are just as important as the shapes of the objects themselves (positive shapes). How these shapes relate to each other (overlapping, interlocking, contrasting) is key to a balanced and interesting design.

The space around and between the objects (negative shapes) is defined (the light areas in A), while shapes have been simplified into geometric (circles and rectangles) and organic (skull) shapes (the light areas in B).

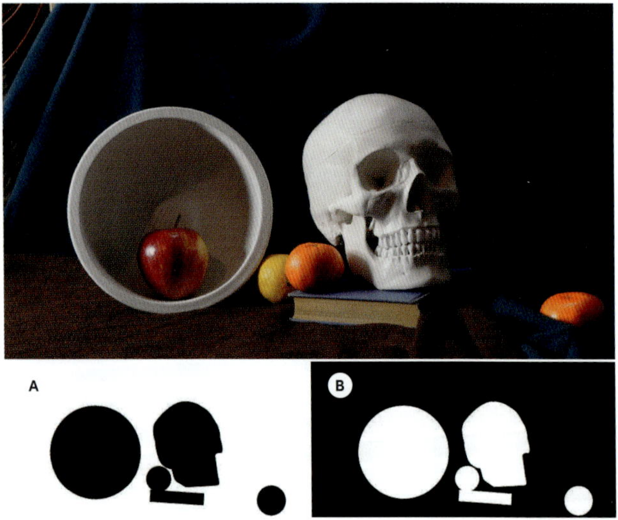

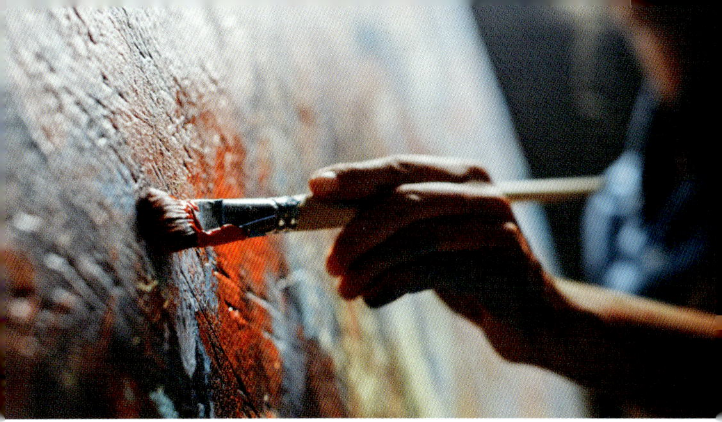

Painting abstractly is a liberating way to explore color and texture. By removing the pressure to make realistic forms, you are free to focus entirely on how these elements interact to build a strong composition.

Values, how light or dark something is, are key to effective composition. Value is what creates the look of form, shadow, and light, making things look three-dimensional. Darker values tend to recede, pushing things into the background, while lighter values advance, bringing things forward. High contrast in values creates drama and adds emphasis, while low contrast is softer and more subtle.

Color in composition generates light, mood, and a sense of space through the control of color harmony, contrast, and saturation.

Texture adds a tactile feel, creates contrast against smooth areas, and can make your painting feel richer and more complex. This can be the actual texture of your paint or the illusion of texture you create.

The Principles of Composition

Now that you know your visual vocabulary, let's talk about the principles—the smart ways you can arrange those elements to create a strong painting. Think of these as flexible guidelines, not rigid rules carved in stone!

Balance is all about making your painting feel stable and harmonious. Visual weight is influenced by things like the size, darkness, color, and complexity of your elements. There are a few ways to consider balance:

- Symmetrical balance is like a mirror image down the middle. It feels formal, stable, and calm. It's great for subjects that need a sense of dignity or stillness, though sometimes strict symmetry can feel a little static.

The composition of "Mead Lines, Winter" is built on symmetrical balance with the tower for the power lines dividing the scene through the middle, with left and right sides balancing each other.

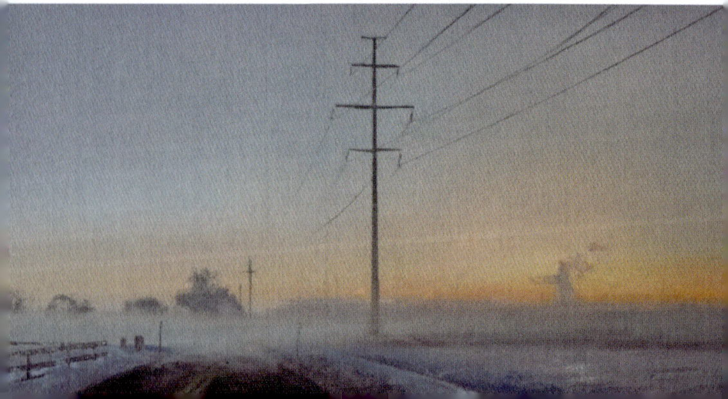

- Asymmetrical balance is more dynamic. You balance elements of different visual weight on each side of an imaginary center line. It feels more natural, active, and less predictable. It's perfect for landscapes or portraits where you want a sense of movement and life.
- Radial balance is circular or seems to radiate out from a central point, like spokes on a wheel or petals on a flower. It draws the eye powerfully to the center and creates a sense of unity and focus.

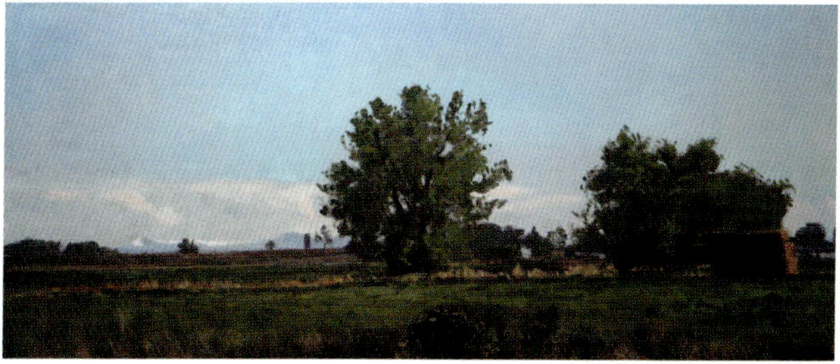

The composition of "Looking South, CR38" is asymmetrical, with the distant mountain on the left balancing the larger foreground trees on the right.

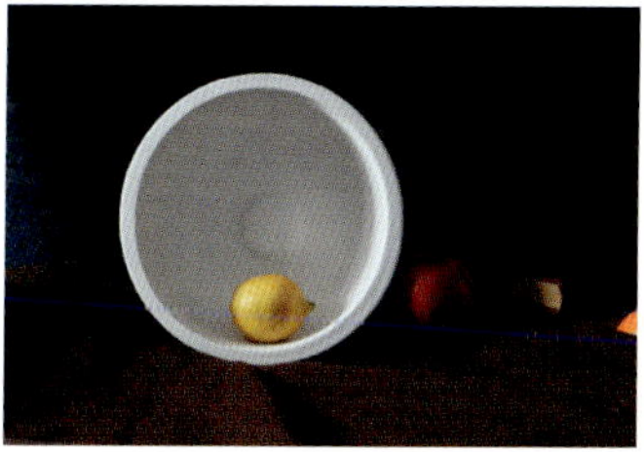

Use a reference photo like this one to construct radial balance in a composition.

Rhythm and movement are about guiding the viewer's eye on pathways through your painting. You can create rhythm by repeating or varying elements like shapes, colors, or lines. Repeating elements creates a visual beat, a sense of order. Varying them—changing their size, shape, or placement—adds interest and creates a flowing sense of movement.

Unity and harmony are about making everything in your painting feel like they belong together, creating a cohesive whole. You achieve unity and harmony by creating connections between elements. Using a limited color palette, or repeating certain colors or shapes throughout your painting, are great ways to tie elements together.

The repeated forms of the palm trees in this composition establishes a rhythm, while the varied spacing and height of the trees creates a melodic quality.

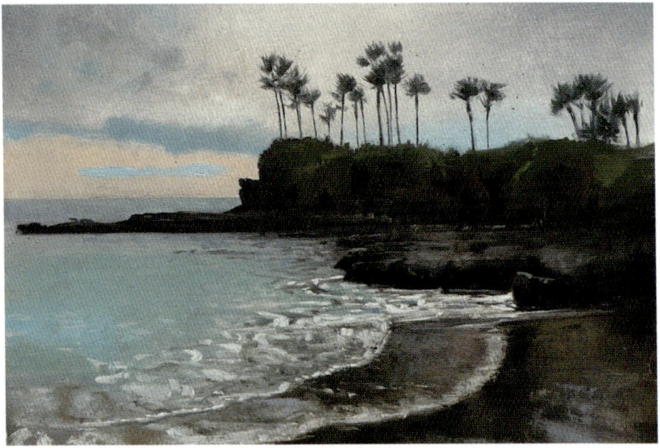

Contrast and variety amplify interest and prevent your painting from being boring. Contrast is all about highlighting differences to grab the viewer's eye and add energy. This can be achieved in a number of ways:

- Value contrast (light against dark) is one of the strongest tools you have for creating drama and directing attention. High contrast is dynamic; low contrast is softer. Use it to create areas of interest and control the tone of your work.
- Color contrast, like placing complementary colors next to each other, creates visual excitement and vibrancy. Warm colors next to cool colors also create contrast and can help with depth.
- Texture contrast, placing smooth next to rough, adds tactile interest and makes surfaces feel more real.
- Size contrast, placing big next to small, creates visual hierarchy and makes certain elements more important.

The intense color of the orange on top of the blue book creates contrast in color, texture, and value.

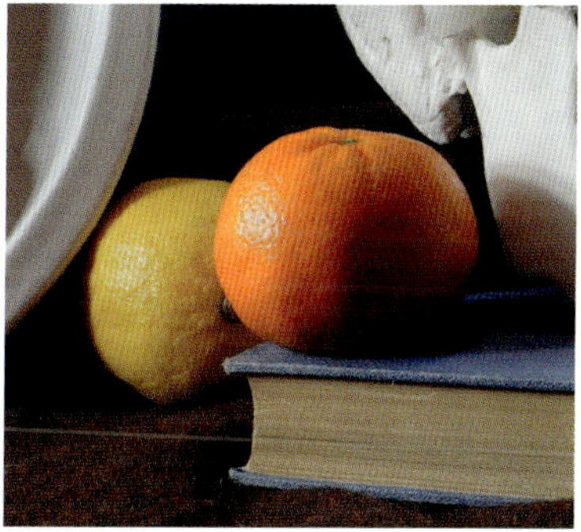

Thumbnail Sketches Walk-Through

The best way to get comfortable with composition is to plan it out before you start painting. This exercise focuses on thinking and planning on a small scale, allowing you to design with intention. Grab a sketchbook, a pencil, and follow me on this four-step walk-through.

THE REFERENCE IMAGE

I start by picking something to paint—maybe a still life setup, a photograph I took, or a view from my window. Before I make a mark, I take some time to scan the scene to familiarize myself with the visual elements. I look for lines, values, colors, and textures that seem compelling. This is my starting point; my goal is to understand the raw materials I have to work with.

IDENTIFY BASIC SHAPES

Next, I look past the details to identify the big, dominant forms. I simplify the scene into basic shapes—circles, squares, triangles, or organic shapes. This helps me to see the underlying pattern of the image, which is critical for a strong composition. By reducing a complex scene into simple shapes, I make the image manageable and easier to manipulate during the planning phase.

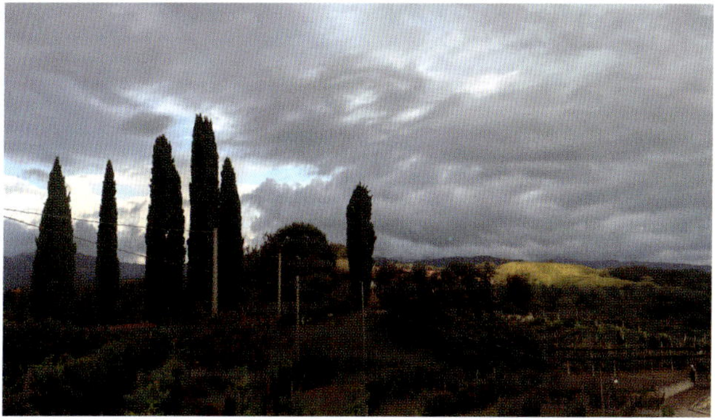

The reference image–this scene has several strong visual elements, which serve as a good example to explore the role shapes play in composition and design.

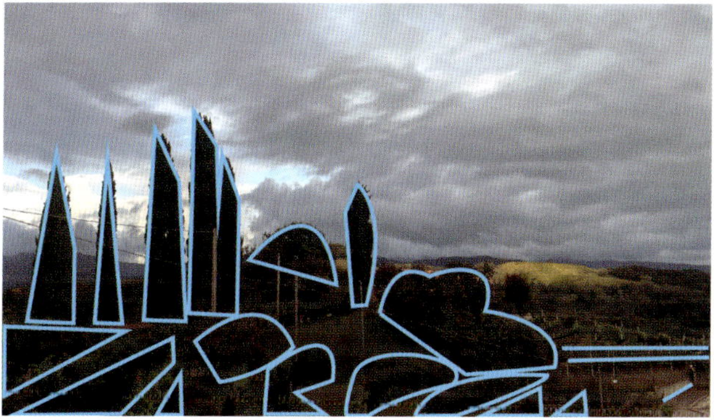

Identify the shape–simplify the shapes that can be seen, and even draw on the reference image if that helps.

USE A VIEWFINDER

I grab a viewfinder, either a store-bought one or two right angles cut from rigid paper. I look at the reference image through the viewfinder and move it around. See how changing the frame changes the picture? I try different sizes and shapes of openings to explore various framing options. I also experiment with different proportions, such as a wide landscape format versus a tall portrait format. This helps me isolate the most potential effective compositions within the larger scene.

TEST WITH THUMBNAILS

Finally, I make at least four to six different thumbnail sketches of the same subject. Time to experiment! I try arranging those simplified shapes and values in different ways. I move the main subject around—putting it in the center, off to the side, or using the "rule of thirds" (imagine a tic-tac-toe grid and place elements where lines intersect).

I assign a value to my shapes, keeping it simple with just three to five distinct values (white, grays, and black). Once I have a bunch of thumbnails, I look at them critically. Which ones feel the most balanced? Does my eye move through the sketch in a pleasing way? I then pick the strongest one to refine.

PRACTICE!

Composition might seem mysterious at first, but it is just a set of tools you can learn. By practicing with thumbnails, you will gain confidence in designing paintings that communicate your artistic message powerfully.

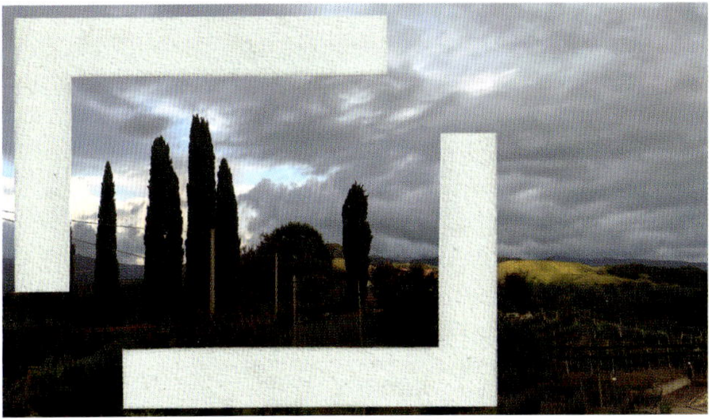

Use a viewfinder–it will help isolate specific compositions within your reference image. Move the frame to test different proportions to see which arrangement creates the strongest design.

Test with thumbnails–by keeping these small and simple, you can quickly compare multiple compositions side-by-side to determine which one offers the best balance and visual flow.

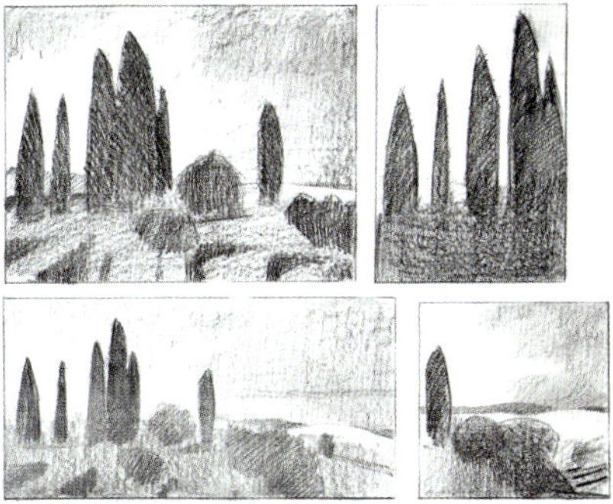

CHAPTER 8

Start Your Painting

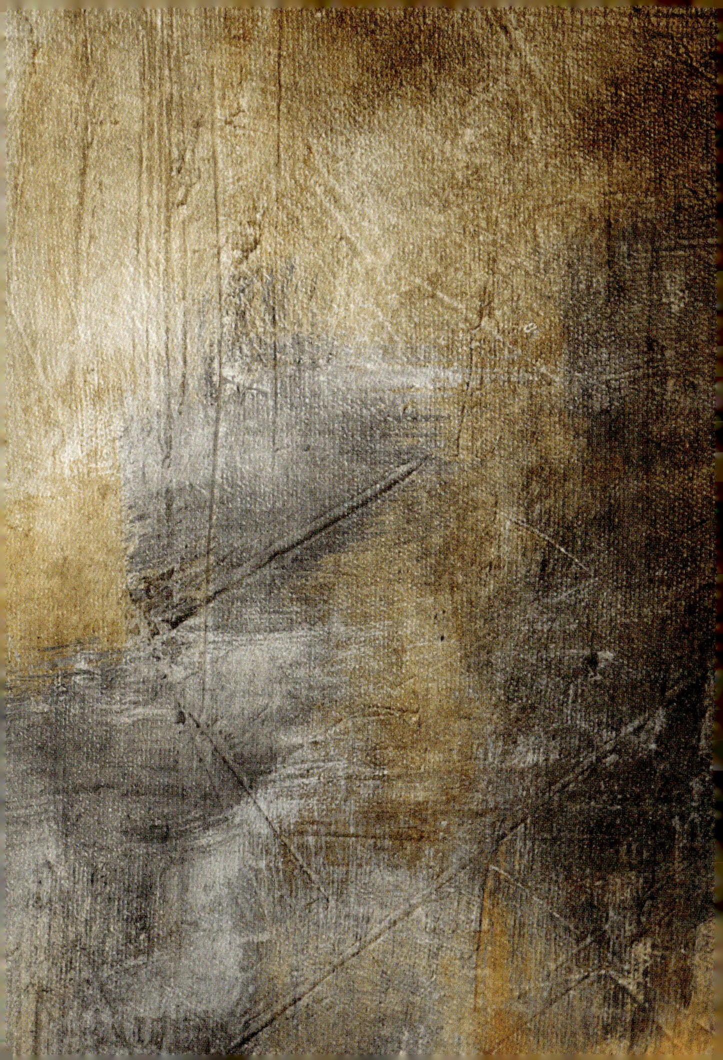

Making Your First Marks

Taking the initial leap can be intimidating, but there are a variety of approaches that can help. From the bold spontaneity of a direct painting approach to the careful preparation of a preliminary drawing, and the tonal control of a grisaille, we'll walk through six different ways to begin, helping you find a method that feels comfortable and confident for you.

Direct Painting

If you have an inclination to be spontaneous and want to capture the energy of a moment, then direct painting, also known as alla prima (Italian for "at first attempt") might be your perfect starting point. This method is all about jumping right in and applying paint directly to your canvas without any elaborate planning or underlayers.

The beauty of direct painting is its immediacy and expressiveness. You apply colors while they're still wet, blending and layering them right there on the canvas. This creates soft edges and smooth transitions, and gives your painting a lively, energetic feel. If you love working quickly and intuitively, letting the painting evolve as you go, this spontaneous approach can be liberating.

There are numerous methods for starting to paint, including direct painting as seen here. No matter which approach you choose, be prepared for the painting to change and evolve throughout the entire process.

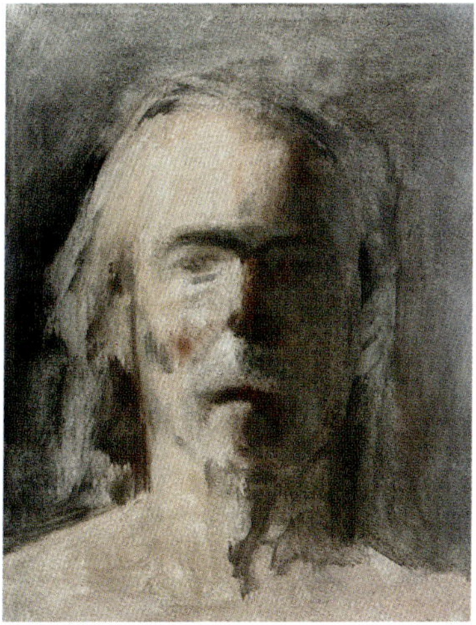

Direct painting captures a moment in time by applying and blending wet paint directly on the canvas and without preliminary underlayers.

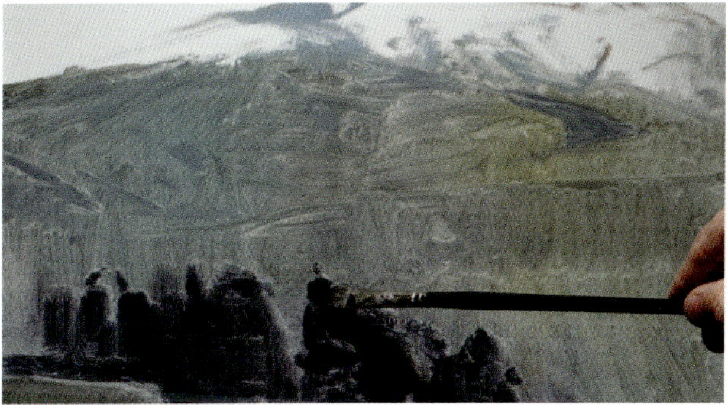

Grisaille

If you prefer a more structured and deliberate approach, or if you want to establish your lights and shadows from the beginning, consider using the grisaille method. This technique involves creating a complete underpainting using shades of gray or a single color like Burnt Sienna or Raw Umber.

A grisaille underpainting lays the groundwork for light and shadow, using shades of gray to build a strong, three-dimensional form before the first touch of color is even applied.

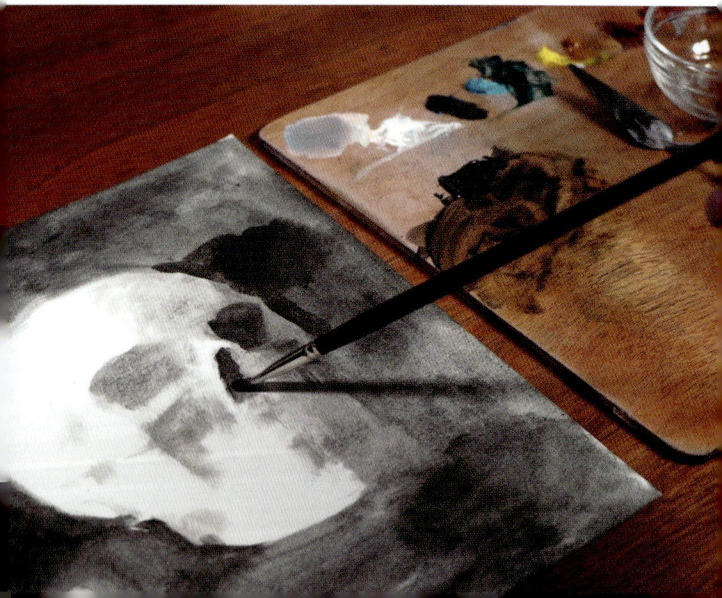

Without getting distracted by color, you build a strong foundation that makes your painting feel solid and three-dimensional. It's like creating a detailed map of the light and shadow before you even think about color. This disciplined approach is excellent for developing your understanding of value and is particularly helpful for subjects where getting the form right is crucial, like portraiture or still life.

Creating a grisaille underpainting is a straightforward process: first, you might lightly sketch your composition onto your canvas with a pencil or thin, diluted paint line. Then, using black (or other neutral hue) paint and white paint, you'll mix a range of gray values, from very light to very dark. Use your brushes and these shades of gray (you can add a little solvent for a smoother flow) to paint your entire composition, focusing on establishing the lights, shadows, and all the mid-tones. Once this grayscale underpainting is complete and thoroughly dry, you'll have a solid foundation of light and shadow ready for you to apply your color layers on top.

TIPS FOR WORKING WITH GRISAILLE

- Keep your paint thin and use white paint sparingly.
- Emphasize design and composition over details.
- Focus on light and shadow shapes.
- Take your time and build in layers.
- Remain open to changes as the painting develops.

Toned Ground

Sometimes, starting with a stark white canvas can feel a little intimidating. That's where a toned ground becomes helpful. This simply means applying a thin, even layer of color to your canvas before you start your main painting. It's a quick and effective way to eliminate the bright white, and instantly sets a mood and influences your color harmony.

A toned ground does a few things. It can help unify all the colors you apply on top, creating harmony. The color you choose for your ground can also influence the temperature of your painting—a warm tone (like a light brown or red-orange) can shift your color mixtures to become warmer, while a cool tone (like a pale blue or green) can shift subsequent paint mixtures to become cooler. In addition, having a mid-tone to work on can make it easier to evaluate your values accurately as you paint. You can apply a toned ground for any subject.

To tone the ground, thin a small amount of your chosen oil paint with odorless mineral spirits or turpentine until it's the consistency of thin ink or watercolor. Dip a brush, a lint-free rag, or a paper towel into this thinned paint and simply rub or wipe it evenly across your entire canvas surface, making sure you cover everything right up to the edges. Build up the color with a second thin layer if needed, and the solvent will help it dry relatively quickly, leaving behind a thin, even veil of color that prepares your surface for next steps.

A toned ground removes the intimidation of a white canvas and unifies the painting's color palette from the very beginning.

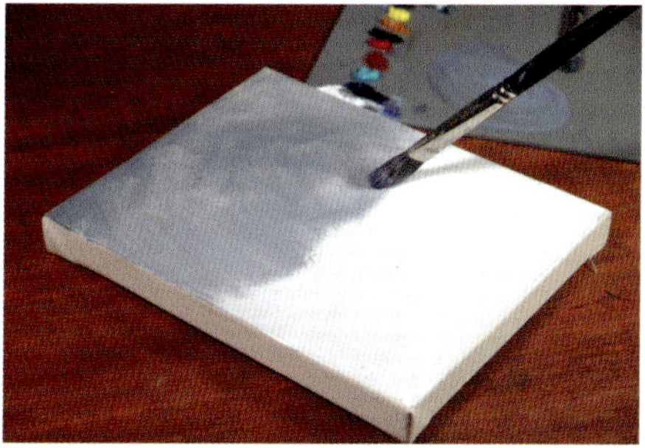

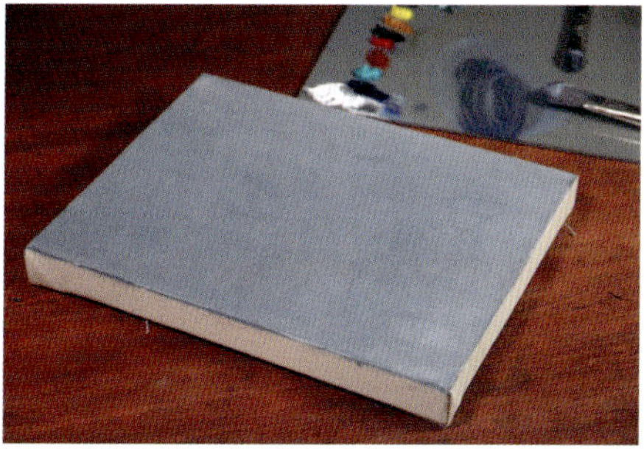

Subtractive

A variation of toning, this begins the same way, applying an even layer of thinned-down oil paint as your toned ground across the canvas. However, while the paint is wet, use a rag or brush and start wiping away areas. This reveals the lighter canvas underneath, creating shapes and areas of light against the darker toned ground. This isn't about drawing fine lines, it's about blocking in larger shapes of light and dark. This subtractive process quickly establishes the big value relationships and compositional structure, giving you a foundation of light and shadow to paint into as you continue working on your piece.

Use a brush or rag to wipe away wet paint on a toned ground to establish the foundational shapes of light and shadow.

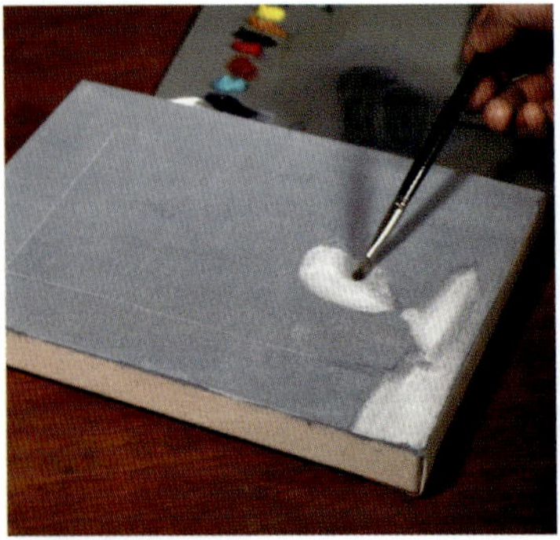

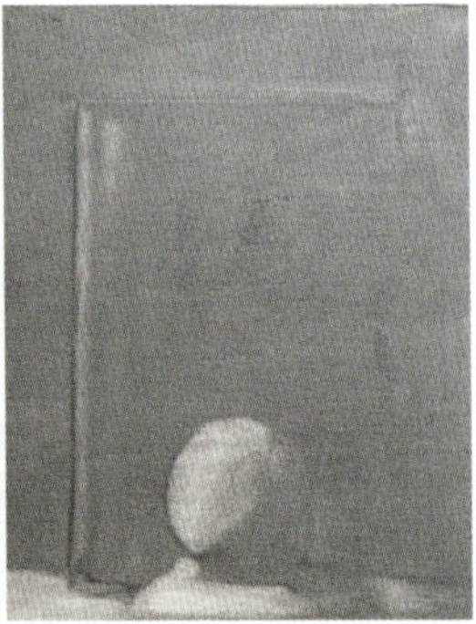

Direct Drawing

Sometimes, you have a specific drawing or sketch you want to ensure is captured accurately on your canvas before you start painting. Or maybe you just feel most comfortable starting with a drawing. One straightforward approach is drawing directly onto your canvas. If you're confident in your drawing skills, you can use a pencil or charcoal to sketch your composition right onto the prepared canvas.

Draw directly onto the canvas to ensure the composition and precise details are captured accurately before painting begins.

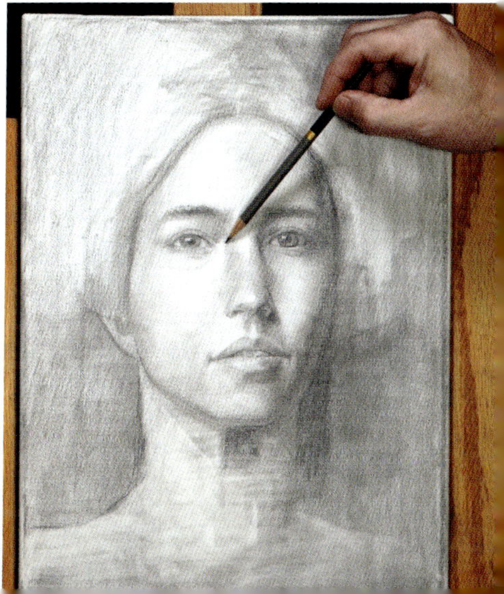

Transfer Techniques

If you have a detailed sketch on paper or are working from a photo reference that you want to replicate accurately, there are various transfer techniques you can use.

THE GRID METHOD

This is a classic: you draw a grid over your reference image and a corresponding grid on your canvas, then transfer the image square by square, using the grid as your guide. It's like connect-the-dots for accuracy and great for resizing images.

The grid method can be modified by using diagonal lines as well, providing an option that requires no measuring. For this method, create diagonal lines connecting the opposing corners of the reference image and drawing. Through the intersection point, run a vertical and horizontal line. From the points at which these horizontal and vertical lines divide the outer edges of the paper, connect them with another set of diagonal lines, which then creates another set of intersection points which can be divided by horizontal and vertical lines.

Use a grid to accurately transfer and scale a reference image, ensuring proper placement and accurate proportion.

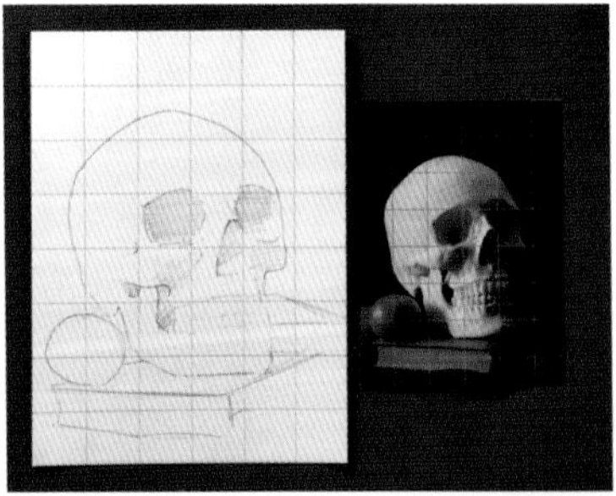

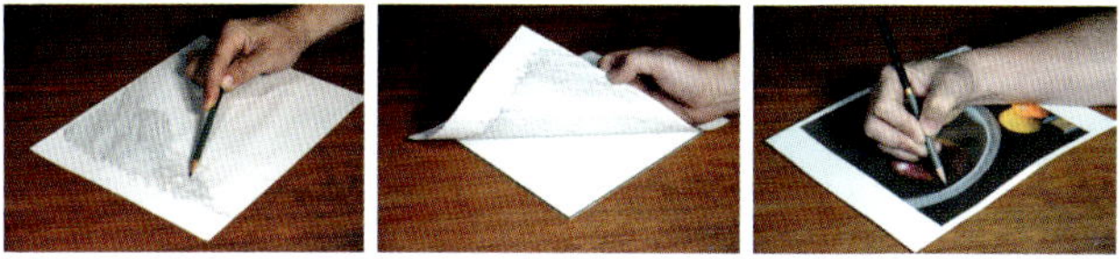

Three steps for graphite transfer: covering the back of a sketch with graphite, placing it on the canvas, and tracing the lines to transfer the drawing.

GRAPHITE BACKING

This is another easy trick: you cover the back of your sketch paper with graphite, place the paper graphite-side down on your canvas, and then trace over your sketch lines with a pencil or stylus. The pressure transfers the graphite onto the canvas as an outline.

For more complex images, or if you have the equipment, a projector can be used—just project your image onto the canvas and trace the key lines directly.

Whichever drawing or transfer method you choose, once your drawing is exactly how you want it on the canvas, give it a light spray with workable fixative (make sure it's suitable for your drawing material). This gives you a clean drawing foundation that stays put as you begin to paint.

Mix and Match

This chapter has given you a peek at several different ways to begin your oil painting. Experiment with these approaches, see which ones feel comfortable and engaging, and don't be afraid to mix and match elements from different methods.

CHAPTER 9

Build Your Painting

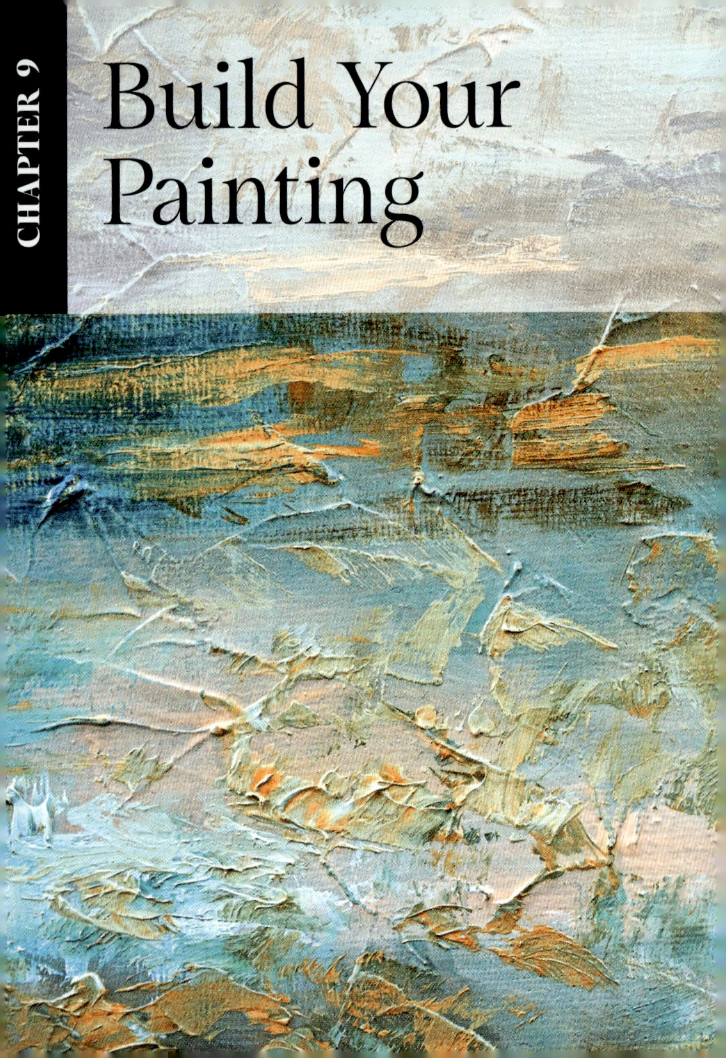

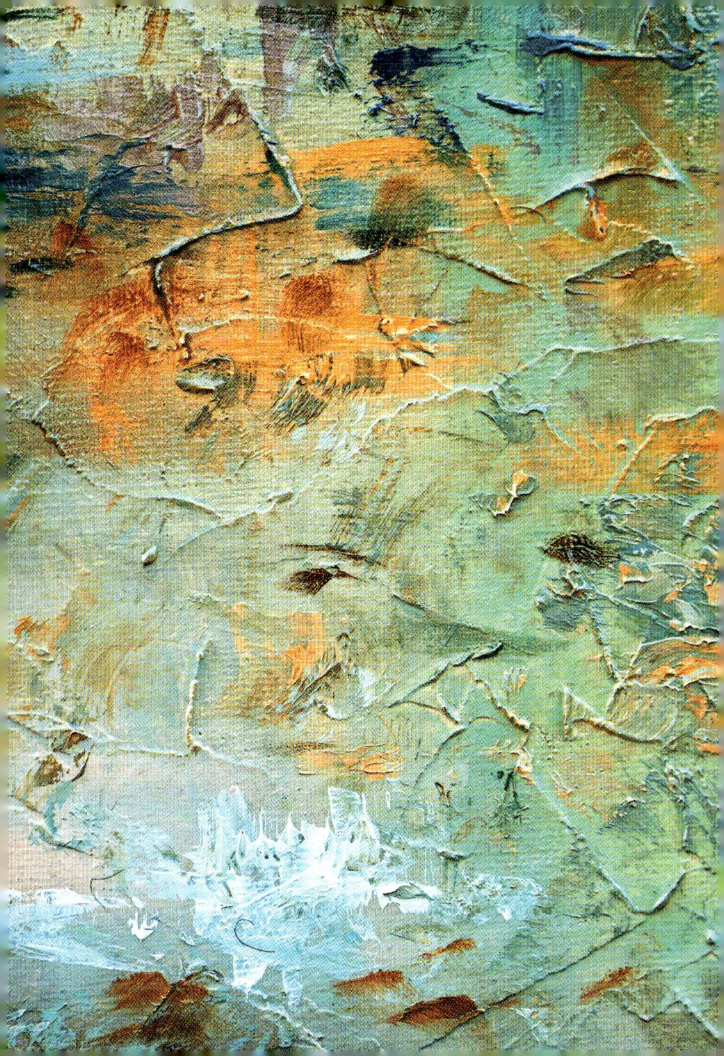

Developing Your Work

Now comes the building up of your painting, adding paint layers, and shaping forms with light and shadow. In the full painting process, this is where you will spend the most time creating a foundation of color and value, making adjustments to the composition, and clarifying your thoughts about the finished painting as you see it take shape. We'll look at key approaches that will help move your painting along.

Blocking in the Foundation

Once your initial drawing or underpainting is set, the next big step is often blocking in your colors. This is where you start covering your canvas with the main colors and values of your composition using broader strokes. Don't worry about tiny details yet!

The goal here is to simplify your composition or subject into larger shapes and masses. Squint your eyes a little and look for the big areas of color and their general lightness or darkness. This helps you establish the overall color scheme and makes sure your main value relationships (the big areas of light, medium, and dark) are working together to create a sense of depth and structure right from the start. Remember the "fat over lean" principle from Chapter 4 and thin your paints with solvent for this stage. It will make them easier to spread, blend, and adjust, and prevents your paint from getting too thick too quickly. As your painting progresses, use less solvent and more oil medium for subsequent layers.

Blocking in the main colors and values will establish the overall composition and depth before adding details.

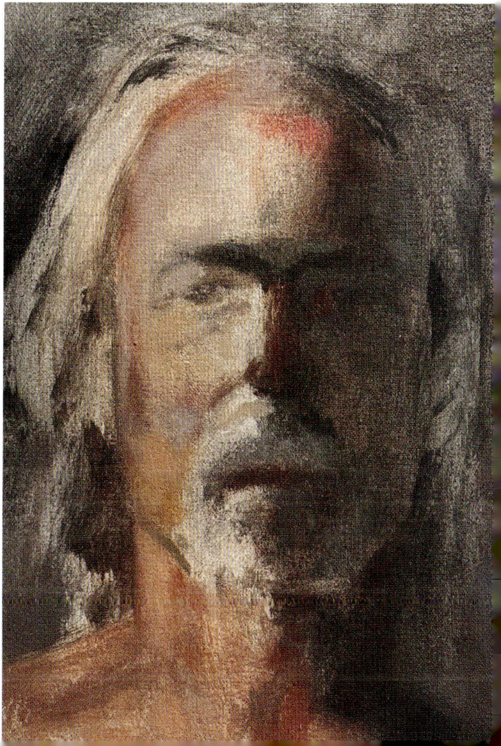

Building Form with Light and Shadow

This is where your painting starts to truly come alive and feel three-dimensional. Light and shadow are essential for creating the illusion of form and volume, transforming flat shapes into objects that look solid and real.

The key to painting convincing form is to simplify what you see. Instead of getting lost in countless subtle shifts in tone and color, train your eye to first identify three fundamental colors for any object.

THE HIGHLIGHT COLOR

Start by locating the light source in your scene. The highlight is the area on the object where that light hits most directly. Crucially, the highlight often reflects the color of the light source itself. For an orange under a cool blue sky, the highlight might be a very pale, whitish-blue. The same orange under a warm incandescent lamp will have a highlight of pale, creamy orange. Note that artificial light can range from cool to warm.

THE AVERAGE LIGHT SIDE COLOR

This is the area that reveals the object's true, inherent color (often called the "local color"). It represents the general color of the side of the object that is illuminated by the light source. For our orange, this would be a vibrant, rich orange. This color is typically deeper and more saturated than the highlight and is often the most intense, pure color you'll see on the object.

THE AVERAGE SHADOW SIDE COLOR

This color represents the entire mass of the shadow side of the object. Generally, this area is darker, cooler in temperature, and less saturated (more muted) than the light side. By mixing one average color for this entire area first, you create a unified shadow shape that helps give the object weight and volume.

By simplifying the orange in this still life into a single average light side color and a unified average shadow side color, the painting effectively establishes a sense of form, volume, and depth.

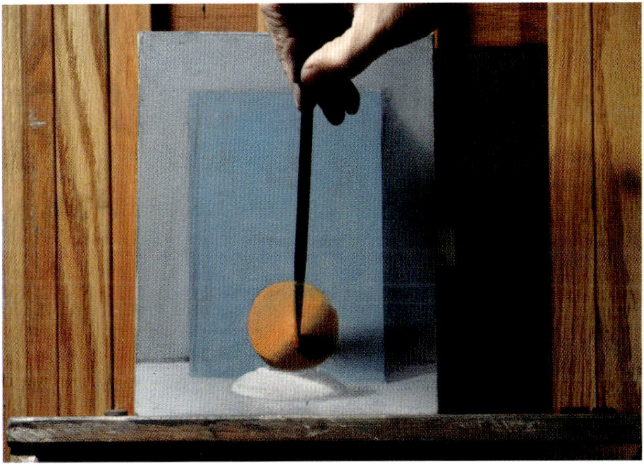

Understanding the Shadow Family

Once you have established the main shadow shape, you can begin to identify its components. Within this shadow mass, you will find three main areas.

THE CORE SHADOW

This is the darkest part of the shadow, located on the form where the light is most obscured (A).

REFLECTED LIGHT

You'll often see light bouncing from nearby surfaces (like a tabletop) back into the shadow side of your object. This is reflected light (B). However, be cautious, as a common mistake is to paint reflected light too brightly. Here's a tip to help: squint your eyes when looking at your subject. When you squint, the reflected light should visually merge with the average color of the shadow area. This tells you that the reflected light is still part of the shadow family—it is much darker and less saturated than you might initially perceive. It is a subtle note of color within the shadow, not a highlight in the shadow.

THE CAST SHADOW

Finally, don't forget the shadow that the object throws onto an adjacent surface. The cast shadow (C) is essential for grounding your object, showing how it sits in space and relates to its environment.

Remember when putting this into practice, to begin with a block-in of an average shadow color. From this solid base, you can then refine the transitions between light and shadow and introduce subtle nuances like reflected light, all without losing the initial sense of form and volume.

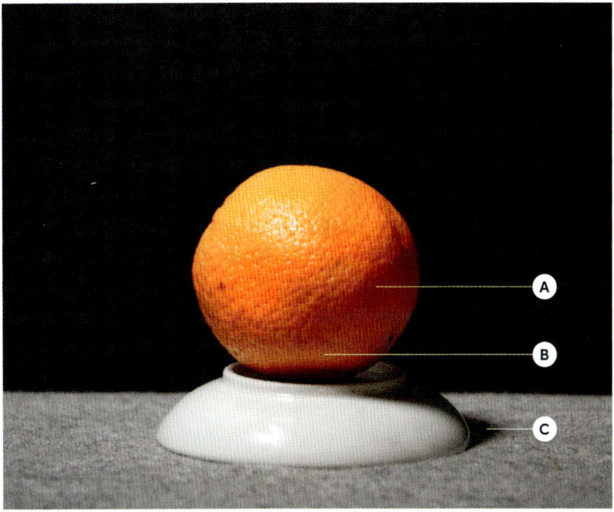

Here, we can see the three main actors in the shadow family: the core shadow (A), reflected light (B), and cast shadow (C).

Painting Wet-in-Wet

One of the distinguishing features of oil paint is its longer drying time, which allows for wet-in-wet painting. This is where you apply new paint layers while the paint underneath is still wet.

Working wet-in-wet allows for blending colors, creating those smooth transitions and beautiful gradients we talked about earlier. The lovely soft edges that this style of painting creates contributes to a sense of atmosphere and unity in your work. It also lets you layer colors and watch them mingle on the canvas, building up depth and complexity in a very fluid way. Embrace the way the colors interact; sometimes the most wonderful effects happen spontaneously when working wet-in-wet!

Working Abstractly

If you're working abstractly, the idea of building forms with light and shadow might connect with you, but the wet-in-wet approach might be more effective. Start moving paint around the canvas, with an emphasis on layering color, scraping, scumbling, exploring texture, and building shapes. Consider a "call and response" approach to painting, in which there are periods of painting that happen freely, followed by periods of painting in which conscious and deliberate decisions are made in response to the freely-made marks.

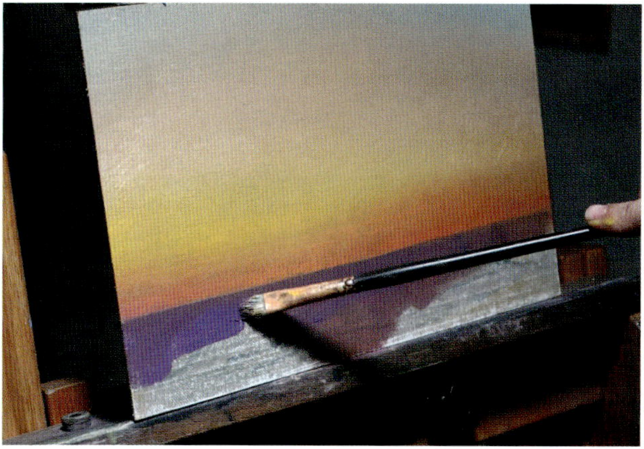

In the initial stage of this landscape study, the lower portion of the painting is applied while the sky in the upper portion is still wet. By carefully merging the two sections of wet paint, the wet-in-wet edge can be softened and manipulated for a distinctive look.

Adjusting and Correcting

Throughout the process, it will be necessary to make adjustments and corrections to your work. Knowing how to correct things confidently is just another skill you'll develop.

If something isn't quite right and the paint is still wet, you can often scrape it away with a palette knife and start fresh in that area. If the paint has dried a bit or you only need a small adjustment, you can simply paint over the area with a new layer of color, as oil paint is often opaque enough to cover what's underneath. For small corrections or to soften an edge, you can also try blending the mistake into the surrounding paint with a brush or knife. And, sometimes what looks like a "mistake" at first, can lead to something unexpected and interesting! Don't be afraid to embrace the process and allow your painting to evolve.

As you practice and experiment with these techniques, you'll start to discover what feels most natural and effective for you. Remember, these aren't rigid rules, but flexible tools you can combine in countless ways. Keep painting, keep exploring, and remain open to new discoveries and experiences.

Artist Insight

The mahlstick, derived from the Dutch "*maalstok*" meaning "painter's stick," has a long and important history. Appearing in paintings of artists as far back as the 16th century, this simple yet effective tool consists of a long stick with a padded or soft leather head. It keeps the painter's hand stable and elevated above the canvas, allowing for greater precision and control, particularly when executing fine details or working on areas that are still wet.

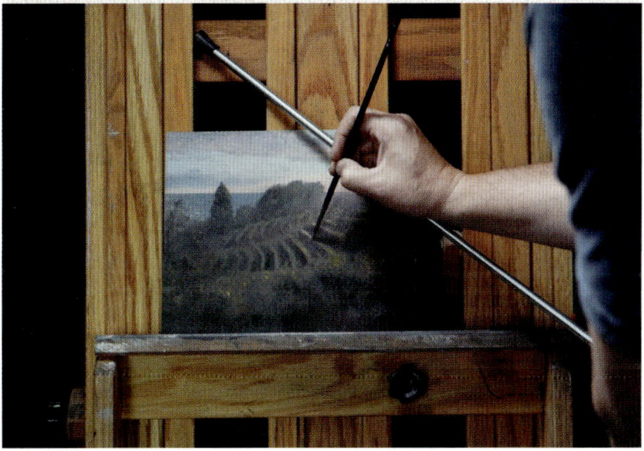

CHAPTER 10

Refine Your Painting

Finishing Touches

You've constructed a foundation, built up your painting, and now it's time for refinement. This is where you bring your painting to completion. It's about adding subtle touches, layers of light, and bits of texture that really make your painting sing and capture the specific feeling or look you're going for.

Adding Details

Details are the final touches that give your painting impact. To use them effectively, you must be selective.

First, identify your area of focus—where you want the viewer's eye drawn to. This could be the sparkle in an eye, the texture of a flower petal, or an intricate pattern. Concentrate your most refined detail work in this zone.

Next, intentionally leave the surrounding areas less defined. This contrast makes your focal point stand out and prevents the painting from looking overly busy or cluttered.

Finally, vary your brushwork for specific effects. Use fine-tipped brushes for delicate lines and accents. Use a stiffer brush to create the impression of texture with broken marks. Adding effective details requires careful observation and patience, but these finishing touches will elevate the realism and character of your work.

Adding highlights to the orange's light side color creates the final sense of form and a convincing three-dimensional appearance.

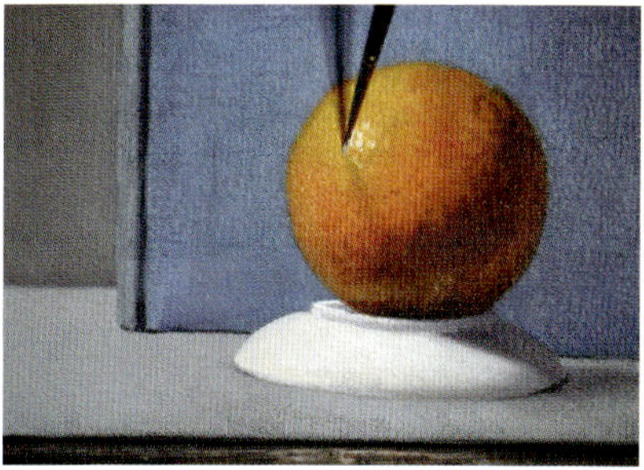

Use selective details to direct the viewer's eye to a focal point while leaving other areas less defined.

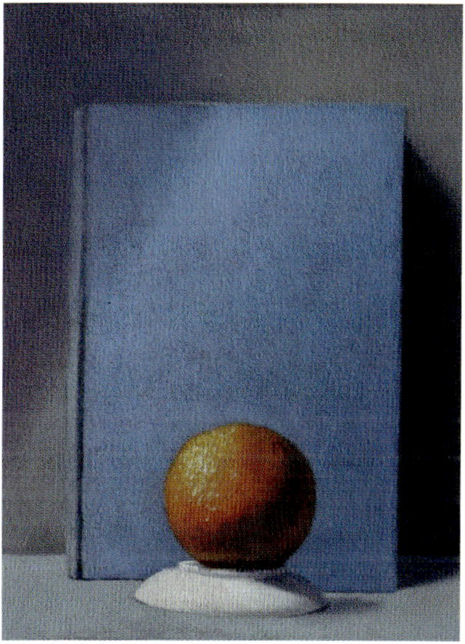

Optical Mixing

Optical mixing is another way of creating visual vibrancy. Instead of physically blending colors on your palette, you place small strokes of different colors right next to each other on the canvas. From a normal viewing distance, the eye blends these colors together, creating a lively, shimmering effect, famously used by the Impressionists. Combining different textures and using optical mixing can add a wonderful richness and vibrancy to your finished painting.

Optical mixing was used selectively here, with small dots of orange and red along the tree line to create a subtle vibration along the edge of the trees. From a distance, these colors blend together, but the impression of color and light remains, helping the trees separate from the blue mountains behind them.

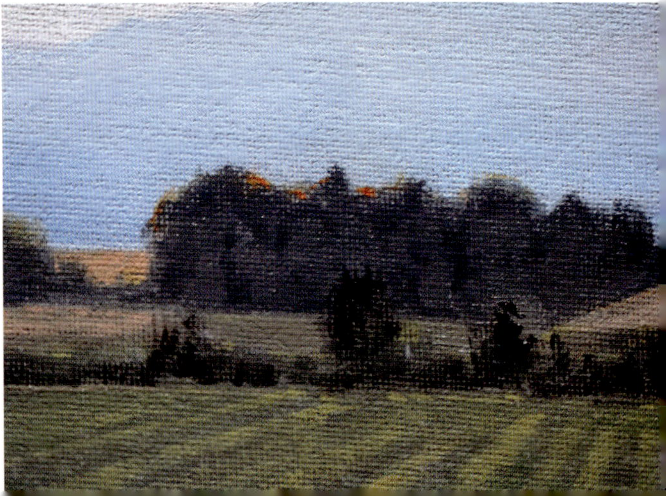

Reworking

Stepping back from a "finished" painting is a critical moment of assessment. You may feel it's complete, or you may realize it needs more work. Whether you need to rework a small area or reconsider the entire piece, oil paint is forgiving. If the paint is still wet, you can easily remove a section by wiping it with a rag, or a stiff brush, and a bit of solvent, giving you a fresh surface to paint over. If the painting is already dry, you can knock down any unwanted texture by scraping the surface with a palette knife before applying new layers on top. Remember, a canvas is rarely a lost cause—it's simply an opportunity for the next stage of your work.

Don't be afraid to scrape down and start over! Sometimes the best results come from "failed" paintings. In both of these examples, there were issues in the paintings that were best resolved by starting again from a smooth surface.

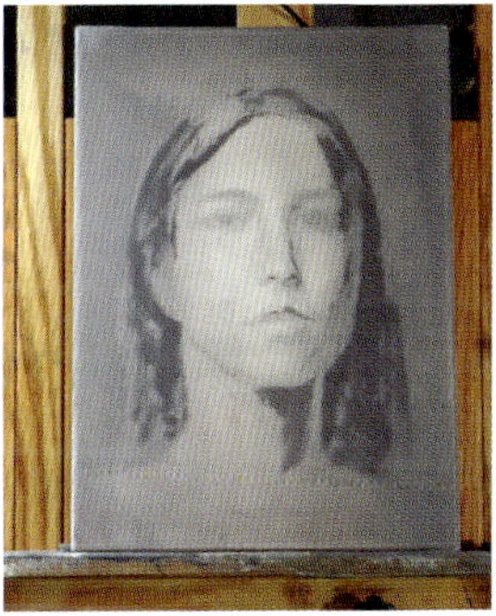

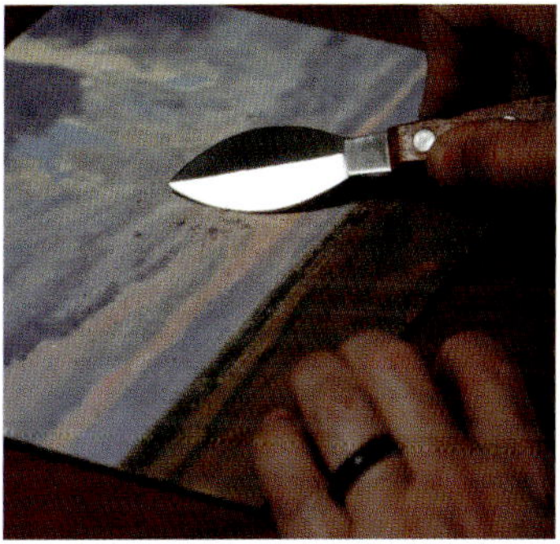

Varnishing

Once your painting is completely finished and thoroughly dry (this can take several months for oil paintings, depending on the paint thickness!), you'll likely want to varnish it. Varnishing does two important things: it protects your painting from dirt, dust, and UV light, and it unifies the sheen across the surface, making your colors look richer and bringing everything together.

Varnishes come in different finishes, from matte (non-shiny) to gloss (shiny), so you can choose one that suits the look of your painting. Apply it in thin, even layers with a soft brush, making sure your painting is totally dry and dust-free first.

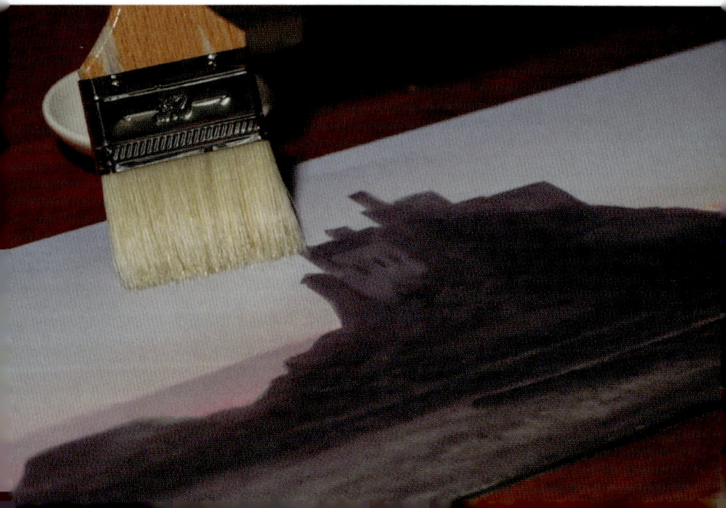

Artist Insight

Throughout the history of oil painting, the choice of natural resins for varnishes significantly impacted a painting's appearance and longevity. Mastic, a popular resin from the Mediterranean, offered a clear, glossy finish but was prone to "blooming" and becoming brittle over time. Its eventual replacement by dammar, a resin from Southeast Asia introduced in the 19th century, marked a shift towards more stable and durable varnishes, reflecting an ongoing effort to improve material properties for both artistic and conservation purposes.

Enjoy the Process

It can be exciting as you get closer to the end of a painting. Rather than rushing to the finish line, allow yourself the space to observe carefully and continue to experiment. Don't be afraid to make mistakes; often, the most interesting discoveries happen when you take a risk with a new texture or glaze. Embrace the journey, trust your instincts, and enjoy the satisfaction of bringing your painting to its conclusion.

Final Thoughts

There's an important thing to remember as you close this book. The real learning, the real magic, happens now, with your brush in your hand and paint on your palette. This book provides a broad look at the tools, techniques, and decisions that are common in oil painting. As you continue to experiment, you'll discover your own relationship with painting—one that you will master as only you can.

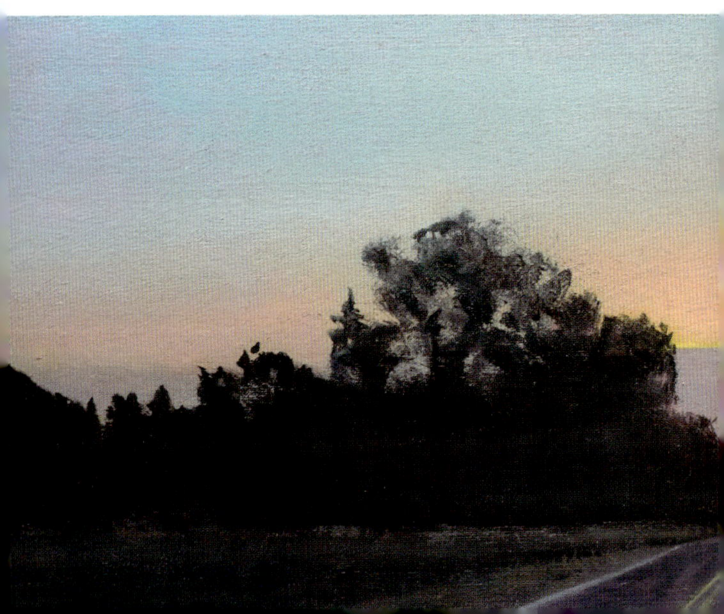

Keep experimenting. Don't be afraid to try new techniques, mix colors just to see what happens, or start a painting in a way you haven't before. Observe the world around you, remain curious, and be open to new discoveries with every "mistake." The more you paint, the more intuitive it will become, and the more confident you'll emerge.

"Mead Lines, Looking East"

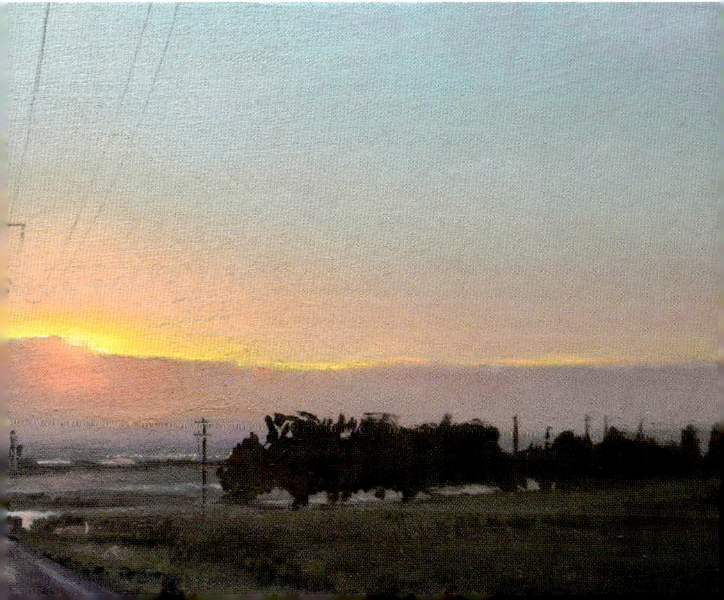

About the Author

Scott Maier is a Colorado landscape painter, who brings the serene beauty of his native Maine coast to his current work in the Rocky Mountains. Inspired by masters like Neil Welliver, James Perry Wilson, and John Singer Sargent, Maier's art is a testament to the power of quiet contemplation and observation. Through a meticulous focus on light and form, he creates immersive experiences that authentically capture the local landscape. With over 25 years of experience, he shares his passion for painting as an adjunct faculty member at Rocky Mountain College of Art and Design, in addition to his extensive background in media production for *Artists Magazine*.

Acknowledgments

I want to thank everyone who has supported me on this path. My sincerest gratitude goes to my parents, who always believed in my artistic dreams. I also want to thank the many teachers and fellow artists who have helped me grow and learn along the way.

To my family and friends, your support has been my strength. Thank you for your love.

Finally, to you, my reader. It's an honor to contribute to your artistic journey, and I'm humbled that you trust me to help you on your way. Remember to trust yourself, never stop learning, and never stop growing. Your work, whether you keep it to yourself or share it widely, is a testament to your existence. It says, "I was here."

INDEX